MOTHERS
OF INVENTION

Ethlie Ann Vare & Greg Ptacek

MOTHERS OF INVENTION

From the Bra to the Bomb:

Forgotten Women & Their

Unforgettable Ideas

WITH A FOREWORD BY JULIE NEWMAR

QUILL
WILLIAM MORROW
New York

Library of Congress Cataloging-in-Publication Data

Vare, Ethlie Ann.
    Mothers of invention : from the bra to the bomb : forgotten women
& their unforgettable ideas / Ethlie Ann Vare & Greg Ptacek ; with a
foreword by Julie Newmar.
        p.   cm.
    Includes index.
    ISBN 0-688-08907-0
    1. Women inventors.   I. Ptacek, Greg.   II. Title.
T36.V36   1989
609.2'2—dc19
    [B]   89-3460
                                                                          CIP

Printed in the United States of America

First Quill Edition

1 2 3 4 5 6 7 8 9 10

BOOK DESIGN BY KATHLEEN CAREY

To our mothers

SHIRLEY HERMAN RILEY
LORIN WADE

from two of their more dubious inventions

FOREWORD

by Julie Newmar

INVENTION IS the pleasure you give yourself when other people's stuff isn't good enough. For me it was looking good when "excellent" still wasn't good enough. It had to be the best, and all I needed to create it was a needle and thread. Simple. The most minimal change in the back seam of a pair of pantyhose took the body from looking flat and artificial to lifted, youthful, and natural. So simple. Why hadn't anyone thought of it before?

No one had, assured the gentleman from the patent office. He blushed profusely throughout our interview, his opaline skin as red as his hair. No wonder he named my invention "Pantyhose with Shaping Band for Cheeky Derrière Relief." Maybe the meaning would get lost in all those nouns.

Really, no woman would know what that was. A potty trainer? A weapon you can use to tie your ratty little sister to the bed?

Something you'd wear on the Via Veneto? Have you seen your posterior lately?

Inventing isn't difficult. You've probably invented twenty household items yourself. It can be done anytime, anywhere. For instance, when you're waiting for the alarm to go off a second time before getting up. Laziness is an excellent virtue.

Boredom is another favorite condition of mine. I've had some great ideas in the worst traffic jams of New York City. Once, a Jacopo Italian vegetable truck almost ran over me while I was discovering the curb.

Borrowing is another good idea—although it's called stealing if the other guy remembered to patent it first. Little comes without reminders from the past.

And being without, being deprived is helpful. Confusion is good, too. Think of it as simply having a profligacy of ideas. Failure I also like. It eliminates leaks. It's very positive to know where not to be.

Invention, discovery, new ideas—such a high. Of course, the highest high I've ever had is from breathing. You think I'm kidding? Try it. Lie down, preferably with some new age music in your ears—Vangelis, perhaps—and breathe deeply, thirty times. Lift the breath out of your throat at the last second, let it fall from an open mouth. Tune in your brain, ask a Higher Source to show you how. I know what I want, but I always leave my senses open as to how it can come to me.

The Infinite Intelligence, the most powerful library, can deliver the answer to you. Most likely, it will come in the form of symbols. I like those high-frequency messages, like minute blips I feel in my solar plexus. Some people call it intuition. It's free for the asking, you know. The clarity of these messages has an ecstasy like none other I've experienced. But you must ask for it.

Also, be very clear, very concise when you address the Infinite Intelligence. And when you get an answer, don't judge it. If you think you're hearing your own voice, like a stuck record, just let it drift from your awareness, like a leaf on the water, flowing under a bridge. Relax, keep tuning in. The chatter becomes unnecessary; the answer comes in symbols, in pictures. This is the formula for

8

invention. Ask it anything. How to change your life; how to deal with your husband. Ask. The answer is already there.

This is the method I use to find something that is lost. After all, nothing is really lost. You simply went somewhere else. I breathe, "My hand is on the key," and I know it will be only a few minutes until my body, like a Geiger counter feeling a warm spot, will reach for where that key is hidden.

What you love is where your attention is. And that's what you get more of.

Go for it! Invent something! I like the idea of getting what you want. Don't you? Let go of judgment and just observe. Pay more attention and you will see that it's always true.

Enjoy.

JUNE 1987
BRENTWOOD, CALIFORNIA

ACKNOWLEDGMENTS

A PROJECT AS AMBITIOUS as the first book on women inventors requires the assistance of many people and organizations. We would like to thank the following institutions and their representatives for their contributions to *Mothers of Inventions* and to apologize to those we've inadvertently omitted:

The U.S. Patent and Trademark Office, the Women's Bureau of the U.S. Department of Labor, the Patent Information Clearinghouse, the Innovation Invention Network, Norman C. Parrish of the National Congress of Inventor Organizations, Susan Boone of the Women History Archives of Smith College, Pat Parrett and Ray Bower of the Carnegie Institution of Washington, the Society of Women Engineers, Ann Forfreedom and the Women's Research and Resource Center, the Business and Professional Women's Foundation, T. A. Appel of the American Physiological Society, the American Statistical Association's Committee on Women in Statistics, Roberta Toole of the Inventors Association of St. Louis, Russell D. Egnor, Anna C. Urband and Patricia W. Viets of the Department of the Navy, Lisa Brower of Vassar College, Carole Manloff of the Melitta Corporation, the Nestlé Corporation, the Gillette Corporation, Maggie E. Weisberg of the Inventor's Workshop International Education Foundation, Nikki E. Godwin of the Bette Clair MacMurray Foundation, the Gihon Foundation, Deborah J. Warner and Bernard S. Finn of the National Museum of American History, Carolyn Kopp of Rockefeller University, Nancy Cuoto of Cornell University Press, Eileen Reilley of the American Chemical Society, Elizabeth Shenton of Radcliffe College, Atlanta University, University of Arizona, American Home Economics Association, Matilda McQuaid of the American Institute of Architects, the Intellectual Property Owners, Memphis State University's Center for Research on Women, the National Women's Hall of Fame, Minnesota Inventors Congress, the Southwest Institute for Research on Women, the Royal Swedish Academy of Sciences, Robert C. Post of *Technology and Culture* journal, the

Acknowledgments

Weekly Reader, the National Society of Black Engineers, Inventors Club of America, Susan Green of the University of Washington at Seattle, Dorothy T. Globus of the Cooper-Hewitt Museum, the Medical College of Pennsylvania, the National Society of the Daughters of the American Revolution, the American Institute of Aeronautics and Astronautics, Professor Margaret Rossiter, and Professor Harriet Zuckerman.

We also want to thank the following individuals for their time and cooperation: Stephanie Kwolek, Ruth Handler, Edie Adams, Countess Stella Andrassy, Betsy Ancker-Johnson, Isabella Karle, Yvonne Slaughter, Donald Saccone, and Michael Nesmith.

In addition, we would like to give special thanks for the following friends and colleagues without whom this project would not have been possible: Madeleine Morel, Karen Moline, Alison Brown Cerier, Andy Ambraziejus, Mary Toledo, Howard Weinstein, Evangeline Griego, R. J. Stevens, Lindsay Brohamer, Fiona Brohamer, Phalen G. Hurewitz, Jill Richmond, Jessica M. A. Speetjens, Shirley Riley, and Professor Anne Fausto-Sterling of Brown University.

Finally, thank you Alisse Kingsley, John Hunt, and Russell Vare for always being there when we needed you, Vicki Radovsky for the initial inspiration, and Julie Newmar for your generosity.

—ETHLIE ANN VARE and GREG PTACEK

Correspondence to the authors should be addressed to:

8306 Wilshire Boulevard
Suite 6005
Beverly Hills, California 90211

CONTENTS

Contents

INTRODUCTION

THE FIRST INVENTOR introduced in every grammar-school primer is Eli Whitney, the genius who invented the cotton gin in 1793. Fact is, Mr. Whitney *didn't* invent the cotton "engine" in 1793—or any other year. Eli Whitney built a device conceived, perfected, and marketed by Mrs. Catherine Littlefield Greene, a Georgia belle who, unlike her Massachusetts-born houseguest, was quite familiar with the cotton boll.

Some accounts have it that Mrs. Greene handed Whitney a virtual set of plans for the cotton gin; others believe she "merely" suggested the idea and financed the work. Either way, Catherine Littlefield Greene somehow got lost on her way to those sixth-grade history texts.

Women have been inventing in America since before there was a United States, and in other parts of the world before there was an America. Catherine Littlefield Greene is not the only innovative lady whose accomplishments have slipped through the cracks. Western society has decreed that women do not invent, despite facts to the contrary, and makes it a self-fulfilling prophecy by overlooking a few of those facts.

Even in our Smithsonian Museum, the painting honoring America's great inventors—"Men of Progress" by John Lawrence Mott, c. 1856—depicts exactly that: men, all white, and all over the age of forty. By 1856 a young widow named Martha Coston had already patented the Navy's signal flare; Ada Lovelace had designed the prototype computer; Mary Montagu had introduced smallpox inoculation; Nicole Clicquot had invented pink champagne and Elizabeth Flanagan the cocktail; and a Madame Lefebre synthesized the first nitrate fertilizer.

Nor can we look back and laugh at nineteenth-century male chauvinism. In his 1957 book *Inventors and Inventions,* C. D. Tuska, then director of RCA patent operations, said: "I shall write little about female inventors . . . most of our inventors are of the male sex. Why is the percentage [of women] so low? I am sure I don't know, unless the good Lord intended them to be mothers. I, being old-fashioned, hold that they are creative enough without also being 'inventive.' They produce the inventors and help rear them, and that should be sufficient."

By 1957 Eleanor Raymond and Maria Telkes had perfected solar heating; Grace Murray Hopper created the basis of computer software; Melitta Bentz invented the modern coffeepot; Mary Engle Pennington developed refrigeration; Margaret Knight invented the square-bottomed bag; Katherine Burr Blodgett patented invisible glass; Gladys Hobby produced the first usable penicillin; Kate Gleason designed the first tract housing; and Hattie Alexander had cured meningitis.

The National Inventors' Hall of Fame in Washington, D.C., boasted a total of fifty-two inductees in 1984; none was a woman. William Coolidge, the inventor of the vacuum tube, is mentioned . . . but not Marie Curie, who invented what we now call the "Geiger" counter and discovered radium. Enrico Fermi makes the grade for building the first atomic reactor . . . but not Lise Meitner, who first created—and named—nuclear fission. Leo Bakeland is honored for inventing Bakelite . . . but not Madame Dutillet, who created cultured marble a century before.

Snubbing women inventors isn't even exclusive to the New World. In ancient Athens, women were forbidden "to study or practice medicine or physic on pain of death." The medieval Church elevated prejudice against female intellect to the point of dogma. The *Malleus* declares, "When a woman thinks alone, she thinks evil." Eighteenth-century scientist and reformist philosopher Immanuel Kant stated: "All abstract reason, all knowledge which is dry, it is cautioned, must be abandoned to the laborious and solid mind of man. For this reason, women will never learn geometry." Fellow freethinker Jean-Jacques Rousseau echoed those sentiments when he wrote: "An inquiry into abstract truths, into the principles and axioms of sciences that render our ideas more general, is not the province of women."

We've tried to go as far back in history as possible to honor great creative women, although without a comprehensive "herstory," many of their contributions still are lost. Our scope is as broad and diverse as possible, including inventions from the ridiculous to the sublime.

Since 1880, the U.S. Patent Office has officially recognized not only mechanical devices as inventions per se, but also substances, techniques, and processes. Today, it would be possible to patent your lab-grown AIDS vaccine, as well as the steps required to produce it, and the special hypodermic needed to administer it.

In this volume, we expand the definition of Inventor to include the Discoverers, those who advanced humankind by recognizing the value of things that were in front of everyone else all along.

The list of female inventors includes dancers, farmers, nuns, secretaries, actresses, shopkeepers, housewives, military officers, corporate executives, schoolteachers, writers, seamstresses, refugees, royalty, and little kids. All kinds of people can and do invent. The idea that one's gender somehow precludes the possibility of pursuing any technological endeavor is not only outdated but also dangerous. In the words of 1977 Nobel Prize winner Rosalyn Yalow: "The world cannot afford the loss of the talents of half of its people if we are to solve the many problems which beset us."

HERSTORICAL DATA

OBVIOUSLY, the inventions of women before recorded history are difficult to pinpoint with accuracy. But oral tradition and anthropological observation regarding the division of labor make it appear likely that women—as opposed to, say, benign and genderless visitors from space—were the first weavers and leathermakers, thereby inventing dyes and tanning. Early implements like the scraper and the awl were undoubtedly created by women. And women were the tribal potters, inventors of the kiln and the clay.

Prehistoric woman would have invented the mortar and the pestle, and Cro-Magnon women are thought to have developed basic chemistry to create the first cosmetics. Women discovered the first botanical medicines and converted cotton and flax into cloth. Women were the first architects, fashioning huts, wigwams, and yurts.

Since many ancient women inventors were enrolled among the gods for their contributions, it is sometimes difficult to differentiate between religious belief and literal accomplishment. The Egyptian goddess Isis is credited with discovering agriculture and planting the first grains. She invented bread and the process of making linen, and she was the first to put a sail on a boat. Also attributed to Isis is the discovery of the Egyptian art of embalming, a process so arcane that it has not been duplicated to this day.

In Greece immortal Pallas Athene was "founder of the plow and the plowman's toil." She is also called *oleoe inventrix*—inventor of the olive—and credited with fashioning both the first musical instruments and the first suit of armor. The Greek goddess of the earth, Ceres, is thought by some historians to be the deification of a mortal queen who lived in Sicily and introduced the populace to plows and leavened bread.

Minerva, goddess of wisdom, is said to have invented spinning and weaving—inventions few anthropologists doubt to have been an achievement of flesh-and-blood women. Even before Pliny wrote that Pamphile of Cea first combed cotton and wove it into cloth, the loom was the provenance of woman. Today, weaving still lends our language its metaphors for womanhood: "distaff" (the cleft stick that holds flax on a spinning wheel) and "spinster," for example.

China's Se Ling-she, wife of Emperor Hwang-te, is credited with the discovery of silk in about 3000 B.C. She, too, was awarded divinity for her invention and is worshiped as the goddess of the silkworm.

Queen Semiramis of Assyria is said to have invented canals, bridges, and causeways. According to Greek historians, she supervised construction of the Hanging Gardens of Babylon.

Cleopatra—who may or may not be the same Cleopatra of romantic legend—is said to have constructed the first still and been one of the earliest alchemists. Two writings that predate chemistry—*Dialogue with the Philosophers* and *Gold-Making*—are ascribed to her.

Written records surviving from 2000 B.C. establish the early chemical discoveries of two Mesopotamian women. Tapputi-Belatekallim and (first part of name lost)-ninu were known perfumers; (. . .)ninu authored a text on perfumery, complete with cookbook-style formulas for chemical compounds.

The Indian empress Nur Mahal—for whose niece the Taj Mahal was erected—is said to have invented the cashmere shawl and attar of roses.

And who could seriously debate the supposition that it was a woman who invented cooking?

True, the majority of these achievements are too obscured by the mists of time to be attributed definitely to any specific individual—of either gender. But there are a few remarkable women of antiquity whose inventions were recorded and whose lives were documented. We can only guess how many of their colleagues were less fortunate.

Maria the Jewess

THE KEROTAKIS

Variously known as Mary the Jewess, Maria Prophetissa, and Miriam the Prophetess, this scientist of the first century A.D. has been misidentified by some biblical researchers as the sister of Moses. Fragments of her writings, the *Maria Practica,* survive in collections on ancient alchemy. She lived and worked in Alexandria.

Maria's inventions all revolved around the laboratory. Her *balneum mariae,* or water bath, is still in use today. Essentially a double boiler, the *balneum mariae* is used to maintain a constant temperature for experimental substances, or to heat reagents slowly and steadily. It is also the prototype for the autoclave. The modern double boiler is, in France, referred to as the *bain-marie*.

Maria also invented a still called the *tribikos*, which may have been the first device for distillation. It was constructed of pottery and copper tubing.

Her most significant contribution to the nascent art of chemistry, however, was the *kerotakis*. This device, a sort of triangular palette, was used as a reflux apparatus for the sublimation of metals. The vapors of arsenic, mercury, and sulfur—vital ingredients in the manufacture of precious metal from base elements, the primary objective of the alchemist—were created and captured in the *kerotakis*. While the quest to turn lead into gold was a vain one, many important scientific discoveries came out of that exercise in futility.

Once, experimenting with sulfur vapor, Maria synthesized a metal alloy coated with black sulfide, a compound still known as Mary's Black.

Hypatia

ASTROLABE, HYDROSCOPE

Hypatia of Alexandria is the earliest woman scientist whose life is well documented; she was also the last scientist of the Golden Age of Pericles, before enlightenment gave way to the Dark Ages. Her martyrdom has had more of an impact on history than her inventions, although the hydroscope itself—the first laboratory instrument to measure the specific gravity of liquids—was a breakthrough.

Born in Alexandria in A.D. 370, Hypatia came into a rarefied intellectual world. Her father, Theon, was a mathematician and astronomer at the Museum at Alexandria, and Hypatia was his prize pupil. She studied in Athens and Italy, and she became a lecturer and writer in the fields of mathematics, philosophy, astronomy, and mechanics. Her classes were attended by students from throughout the known world, and her treatise on algebra, *Arithmetica,* was a thirteen-volume definitive study.

Practical technology was Hypatia's main interest, which led to her invention of the plane astrolabe, used to measure the positions of the sun and stars and to calculate the ascendant sign of the zodiac. It consisted of a pair of rotating discs made of open-work metal, rotating one on top of the other around a removable peg. Hypatia perfected the device to the point where it could accurately solve problems in spherical astronomy.

She also invented a device for measuring the level of water and another system for distillation, as well as the hydrometer. The hydrometer—or hydroscope—was a sealed tube about the size of a flute, weighted at one end. The depth to which the hydrometer sunk in a particular liquid gave a reading on the substance's specific gravity.

Hypatia never married, although she was courted by and kept company with many of Alexandria's movers and shakers. Unhappily, these connections did not save her from the fanatical Christian sects whose influence was becoming increasingly felt. During her lifetime, intellectualism gave way to fundamentalism, and the true believers were convinced that scientific study was antithetical to religious dogma. In A.D. 389 the Serapeum Library was sacked and burned by order of Theophilos, bishop of Alexandria. All neo-Platonists were persecuted, and Hypatia became a controversial figure because of her fame and influence.

In A.D. 412 Cyril, the patriarch of Alexandria, vowed to rid the city of neo-Platonist "heretics." Hypatia was urged by her friends to renounce her thinking—and her teaching—but she refused. In March of A.D. 415, a group of overzealous monks took Cyril's ranting to heart and murdered Hypatia for her beliefs.

Socrates Scholasticus described the scene: "They pull her out of her chariot, they hale her to the church called Caesarium; they strip her stark naked; they raze the skin and rend the flesh of her

*Hypatia of Alexandria (c. A.D. 370–
415). A martyr to feminine intellect.*

body with sharp shells, until the breath is departed out of her
body; they quarter her body, they bring her quarters unto a place
called Cinaron, and burn them to ashes."

It would be a thousand years until the world saw a rebirth of
the pure science that Hypatia stood for . . . and died for.

Trotula

MEDICAL INNOVATOR

In the eleventh century A.D., Trotula of Salerno—wife of John Platearius—was the preeminent physician, male or female, working and writing in Italy. Her *Practica Brevis* and *De Compositione Medicamentorum* were copied by hand by generation after generation of healers for four hundred years and remained in print for another three hundred years after that. She was the first physician on record to promote cleanliness, a balanced diet, exercise, and avoidance of stress for health maintenance, and she was among the first to prescribe cures that didn't include astrology, prayer, or superstition in the formula.

Trotula was a member of the noble Ruggiero family from the Naples area, but little authoritative information remains about her personal life. Her husband, also a physician, was variously known as John, Johannes, or Giovanni Platearius or Platerio; their sons, Matthias and Johannes the Younger, were both medical writers in their parents' footsteps. Trotula probably died at Salerno in about 1097. She would have been trained at home, and been allowed to practice because of the threat of the Black Death and the shortage of trained practitioners of any gender or discipline. Europe was only barely emerging from the Dark Ages.

The Catholic Church prohibited dissection of the human body when Trotula studied and taught, so she learned to diagnose by analyzing skin tone, pulse, facial expression, and urine. Her cures consisted mainly of herbal tinctures and salves, medicinal baths, and bleeding. Surgical techniques included lancing and performing Cesarean sections. According to medical opinion as late as the 1930s, Trotula's medical innovations were "commonsense, practical, up-to-date for [their] time. . . . No book so good of its kind has ever been written, and none followed it for centuries," according to Dr. Kate Hurd-Mead's 1930 text, *Isis*.

Trotula was the first to stitch a perineum after a difficult childbirth, and she introduced support for the perineum during labor to help keep it from tearing in the first place. Her treatises on postpartum care for mother and child were invaluable, and she was the first to address the medical needs of women specifically in her work *Passionibus Mulierum Curandorum—(The Diseases of Women)*, later known simply as *Trotula Major*.

Historians in the years following Trotula's death often inadvertently—or, perhaps, intentionally—credited her volumes to others. The most common translations automatically gave her name the male form, Trottus, and a widely distributed version printed in the sixteenth century credited the books to a male physician named Erotian.

In daring to practice medicine during her time, Trotula was not only an exception to the rule, she also was literally taking her life in her hands doing so. Ignorance ruled the Dark Ages, and superstition the Middle Ages. A woman who attempted the healing arts was considered, literally, a "witch doctor"—and many of the infamous witchcraft trials of the period punished women for nothing more than infringing on a male-dominated "craft."

Tens of thousands of women throughout the Middle Ages were burned at the stake as witches. It's estimated that an average of two "witches" *a day* were executed in Germany alone between 1400 and 1600. At Toulouse, France, four hundred witches were put to death in a twenty-four-hour period—accused not of harming people, but of enlisting the Devil's aid to heal them.

A little knowledge is a dangerous thing, goes an old cliché. For a woman before the Renaissance, it could be deadly.

Maria Gaetana Agnesi

CALCULUS

The "witch of Agnesi" isn't a person; it's a mathematical formula describing a curve that solved an age-old conundrum, how to duplicate precisely the volume of a cube. It was developed by the noted linguist and theorist Maria Gaetana Agnesi, whose mathematical savvy was so startling in its time that she earned the appelation the "witch of Agnesi"—and her formula still bears the name.

Maria was no witch. She was, however, the author of *Instituzioni Analitiche (Analytical Institutions)*, the standard mathematical text that helped establish the beginnings of what we now call integral calculus; it was used in all higher education for a century after her death.

Born in Milan in 1718, Maria Agnesi was a child prodigy. By age five she spoke fluent French, and by age eleven she could translate Greek, Latin, German, Spanish, and some Hebrew. Her defense on the education of women was published when she was nine, and her first volume on differential calculus was published when she was twenty.

Maria was first taught the principles of mathematics at home by her father; by 1750 she was nominated to fill his chair in mathematics at the University of Bologna. Her mental acuity bordered on the mystical, according to her biographers: Often she would awaken from a deep sleep and write down the solution to a problem she had been working on earlier in the day. When she awoke,

29

she expressed surprise that the conclusion was detailed on paper by her desk.

The publication of *Analytical Institutions* in 1748 cemented Maria's reputation. Empress Maria Theresa sent her a casket of jewels in recognition, and Agnesi would have been made a member of the French Academy of Science had their rules allowed women in the organization. She turned down the University of Bologna appointment—made by Pope Benedict XIV—because she didn't want to leave Milan. After completing her three volumes on calculus, she retired from intellectual pursuits to devote her life to caring for the poor and sick of her city.

Agnesi converted her home into a public hospital and for the last fifteen years of her life administered the Pio Alberto Trivulzio, a public institution for care of the elderly and homeless. She died at age eighty-one, in 1799, eulogized as a pious benefactress. Her works remained as groundbreaking theses in the nascent field of higher mathematics and set the stage for such acclaimed mathematicians as Emmy Noether, her twentieth-century spiritual daughter who created modern abstract algebra.

Mary Kies / *Mrs Samuel Slater*

FIRST AMERICAN PATENTS

Mrs. Mary Kies of South Killingly, Connecticut, is erroneously credited as the first woman to be granted a patent in the United States of America. The patent for "a method to weave straw with silk and thread" was granted on May 5, 1809, and was in use for about ten years in the heyday of the straw bonnet. However, the first patent granted to a woman in the United States was to Mrs. Samuel Slater in 1793 for cotton sewing thread. It not only came earlier, but also was a far more significant invention in terms of general usefulness and longevity. However, Mrs. Slater has been totally overshadowed in memory by her husband, and the person behind this important invention has been all but lost to history.

Samuel Slater himself was a British mechanic who immigrated to America in 1789 and bought a struggling cotton mill in Rhode Island. Thanks, presumably, to his wife's invention, Slater's mill became a prosperous one, and Samuel Slater & Co. soon opened textile mills in Massachusetts, Connecticut, and New Hampshire as well. The mills prospered for three decades at least, leaving Samuel a wealthy man and, it is hoped, bringing prosperity to the woman who made it possible.

Sybilla Masters

COLONIAL CORN

If Mrs. Samuel Slater was the first woman to be granted a U.S. patent (in 1793), she was years away from being the first woman inventor in America. Sybilla Masters, a Quaker raised in the colony of West New Jersey, received English Patent No. 401 on November 25, 1715, for a machine to prepare Indian corn. (England was the first country to formalize the concept of patents, doing so in 1624.) Of course, the paperwork itself was made out to Thomas Masters, Sybilla's husband; but the document clearly credits "a new Invencon found out by Sybilla, his wife."

Sybilla Righton (sometimes recorded as "Sabella" or "Isa-

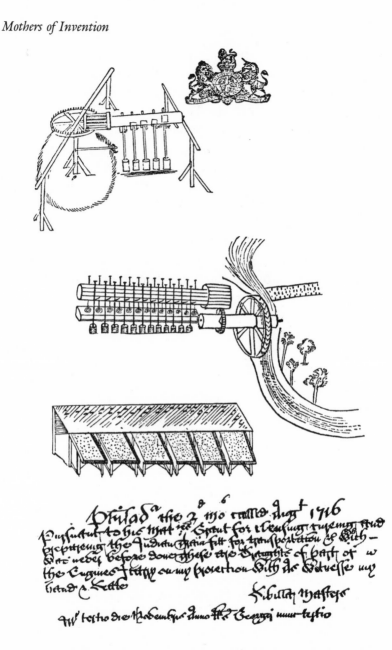

Drawings accompanying the first patent issued to an American. In 1715, colonist Thomas Masters secured British patent #401 for "a new Invencon [sic] found out by Sybilla, his wife." These patent application mechanical drawings are signed by the inventrix herself.

bella") moved from West New Jersey to Philadelphia in the early 1690s, when she married wealthy merchant Thomas Masters. Thomas was a large landowner, mayor of Philadelphia (1708), and provincial councillor (1720–23).

In 1712 Sybilla traveled to England with the express purpose of patenting her refining process for maize—or Tuscarora rice, as she called it—and making her fortune by marketing it abroad. It was her opinion that the hominylike meal was a restorative for "consumptive and sickly persons." The machine she designed to prepare the corn differed from other mills of the day in that it worked on a premise of stamping, rather than grinding, the grain. The combination of wooden cogwheels, mortars, and drying trays could be powered by horse or water; in fact, Thomas bought Governor's Mill in Philadelphia specifically to produce Tuscarora rice.

The Masters patent covered "Cleaning and Curing the Indian Corn Growing in the severall Colonies in America within England, Wales and Town of Berwick-upon-Tweed, and the Colonies in America."

Unfortunately, Tuscarora rice was not embraced by the British, and Governor's Mill continued to be a white elephant handed down from generation to generation. Sybilla, however, had other ideas to work on.

On February 18, 1716, Thomas Masters received yet another English patent, No. 403, for an invention created by his wife. This was "for the Sole Working and weaving in a New Method, Palmetto, Chips and Straw, for covering hats and bonnets, and other improvements in that ware." Ever the businessman, Thomas applied for and was granted a monopoly on the importation of palmetto leaves from the West Indies.

Sybilla set up shop in London, where she sold hats, bonnets, "child-bed baskets," and matting made of the fiber. This enterprise lasted about a year, after which the couple returned to Philadelphia. On July 15, 1717, the Provincial Council granted permission for recording and publishing Sybilla's patents in Pennsylvania.

Governor's Mill continued to produce Tuscarora rice—cornmeal—for the citizens of Philadelphia, although it was the family's enormous property holdings that constituted the bulk of the estate left to their four children. Sybilla Masters died in 1720, Thomas in 1723. It would be seventy-three years until another American woman could officially call herself "inventor."

A WOMAN'S WORK . . .

Everyday Ingenuity

NOT EVERYONE CAN invent oxygen (although that was, in fact, codiscovered by a woman); someone's got to invent the disposable diaper and the brown paper bag. Because the job classifications "domestic servant" and "housewife"—they seem synonymous at times—have traditionally been the main employment of women, it's not surprising that a preponderance of inventions by women pertain to household maintenance. As late as the 1940s, the top four job descriptions for American women were domestic servant, laundress, cook, and seamstress.

Hundreds of innovations, from toasting racks (Mary Evard) to "monthly protectors" (Gertrude Campbell) to portable lunch heaters (Maria Bradley) could be included here; a Margaret Colvin of Battle Creek, Michigan, pattented no less than half a dozen automatic washing machines. The once ubiquitous Bissell carpet sweeper was named for its inventor, Anna Bissell. In 1950, when clerical employment outstripped home economics as the leading occupation of women, the pink-collar corps began to invent things that would ease the drudgery of typing and filing—like Bette Nesmith Graham's lucrative Liquid Paper.

Child care obviously is a major concern for women inventors. Just recently, three Frenchwomen—Dominique Peignoux, Yvette Guys, and Françoise Dekan—began marketing the "Babylodie," a device that is tucked in an infant's diaper and begins to play "When the Saints Go Marching in" as soon as it gets wet. Mommy hears music, Mommy changes baby. (Some fear the invention could lead to embarrassing situations for grown-ups accidentally exposed to the wrong notes.) Also the product of feminine inventiveness are baby carriers, baby jumpers, baby clothing, and potty seats.

If a woman's place is in the home, as diehard male chauvinists would have it, no one can stop them from improving their surroundings.

Bette Nesmith Graham

LIQUID PAPER

Bette Nesmith Graham was a perfect example of necessity as the mother of invention. She founded what was to become a multimillion-dollar enterprise because she was a poor typist. Rather than lose her job, she "cheated" on her typing pool assignments by covering up her mistakes with white paint. By the time of her death in 1980, Liquid Paper was a worldwide corporation and the staple of offices everywhere; Bette left a $50 million fortune. The fact that half the money went to her son, former Monkee Michael Nesmith, is one reason music video is so popular today. Michael invested his inheritance in Pacific Arts Studio, a forerunner in the production of video music.

Bette Nesmith Graham was born Bette Claire McMurray on March 23, 1924, in Dallas, Texas, to an auto wholesaler and a housewife who dabbled in painting, singing, and needlework. Her sister, Yvonne, remembers Bette as "strong-willed and determined to do her own thing." Always a discipline problem in school, Bette dropped out at seventeen and applied for a job as a secretary in a law firm—even though she couldn't type. The firm liked her spirit, though, and sent her to secretarial school. In the evenings, she earned her high-school diploma.

In 1942 Bette married her high-school sweetheart, Warren Nesmith, and their son Michael was born on December 30, 1943. By this time, Warren was off to war. Bette became a single, working mother at age nineteen. Since the Nesmiths divorced shortly after Warren's return from the service in 1946, that status was to last until she married Bob Graham in 1964.

By 1951 Bette Nesmith had managed to provide a home for herself and her son and had worked her way up the career ladder to a position as executive secretary at the Texas Bank & Trust in Dallas. And this is where her hastily learned secretarial skills got her into trouble. The new IBM electric typewriters, with their carbon film ribbons, left a terrible mess behind when you tried to erase a typographical error.

"I remembered trying to make a little extra money by helping design the holiday windows at the bank," recalled Nesmith. "With lettering, an artist never corrects by erasing but always paints over the error. So I decided to use what artists use. I put some tempera waterbase paint in a bottle and took my watercolor brush to the office. And I used that to correct my typing mistakes."

For almost five years, Bette would sneak her bottle of white paint out of the drawer and correct her typos. It was considered cheating, a way of passing herself off as a better typist than she was. Once, when she changed jobs, her new boss admonished her, "Don't use any of that white stuff on my letters."

By 1957, young Michael Nesmith was helping mother, Bette, fill one hundred bottles of "Mistake Out" in their garage. Michael would later become a pop star; Bette Nesmith would become a millionairess; and "Mistake Out" would become Liquid Paper.

The boss might not have approved, but the gals in the typing pool knew a good thing when they saw it. After the umpteenth coworker asked Bette for a bottle of her magic potion, she went home and made the first batch of what the handpainted label called "Mistake Out." In 1956 she had a cottage business going, supplying bottles of Mistake Out to secretaries at Texas Bank & Trust. Later that year she was encouraged to market the product publicly. She changed the name to Liquid Paper and began the tedious job of trademarking and patenting the product. First, however, she decided to improve the formula.

"I went to the library and found the formula for a type of tempera paint," she recalled. "A chemistry teacher from Michael's school helped me a bit. I learned how to grind and mix paint from a man at a paint manufacturing company."

Using her kitchen as a lab and her garage as a bottling factory, Bette worked nights and weekends perfecting a quick-drying, undetectable, cover-up fluid. She offered it to IBM, which declined. She decided to market it herself.

By the end of 1957, Liquid Paper was selling a hundred bottles per month—bottles that were filled out of squeezable ketchup and mustard containers by young Michael and his friends in the family garage. After an article about the product appeared in a national office supply magazine, the hundreds of bottles became thousands of bottles. Yet Bette kept her day job until the morning she was fired for accidentally typing "The Liquid Paper Company" on the bottom of a letter—instead of her employer's name.

It took a long time for "The Liquid Paper Company" to become profitable. In 1966, Michael was earning far more as a member of television's "prefab four" than his mother was as owner and founder of Liquid Paper, Inc. And then things started to take off. In 1968 Liquid Paper grossed more than $1 million, producing in excess of ten thousand bottles a day.

In 1975 Liquid Paper employed two hundred people, produced twenty-five million bottles of the stuff, and distributed it to thirty-one countries. Bette Nesmith resigned as chairman of the board, vowing to devote the rest of her life to her charities, religion, and art. In 1979 the Gillette Corporation bought Liquid Paper for $47.5 million—plus a royalty to Bette Nesmith Graham on every bottle sold until the year 2000. When she died on May 12, 1980, Bette Nesmith Graham left half her fortune to her son and half to her philanthropic foundations.

Melitta Bentz

DRIP COFFEE

In 1908 a housewife in Dresden, Germany, became annoyed with the time-consuming method of brewing coffee by wrapping the loose grounds in a cloth bag and boiling water around it. Worse, coffee made that way (or by the shortcut of boiling coffee grounds right in the water) was bitter-tasting and grainy.

So Melitta Bentz ripped a sheet of blotting paper from her son's schoolbook, cut a circle of the porous paper, and stuck it in the bottom of a brass pot that she had poked full of holes. She reasoned that if she put the coffee grounds on top of this filter and poured the boiling water over it, she could get the taste of the coffee without the bad side effects.

Melitta Bentz was right about the coffee filtration system—so right, in fact, that she and her husband, Hugo, hired a tinsmith to produce the newfangled coffee pots for sale. In 1909 they brought their drip system to the Leipzig trade fair and sold more than twelve hundred "coffeemakers," as they called them. The Melitta company was born.

By 1912 Melitta was manufacturing its own line of coffee filters. Frau Bentz's company continued to grow, owned and operated by her children and her children's children. Her original disk-

42

*The all-but-generic name "Melitta filtered coffee" is actually a nod
to the system's inventor, Melitta Bentz, shown here with her original pot.*

shaped filter was replaced by the familiar cone shape of today, and
early metal pots were replaced by porcelain and plastic models.
The Melitta coffeemaker is used today in 150 countries worldwide;
two thirds of American coffee drinkers use the drip preparation
method.

From a cottage in Dresden and a *Hausfrau* with a taste for
good coffee grew an international concern and a woman's first
name that will forever remain synonymous with this omnipresent
appliance.

Marion Donovan

DISPOSABLE DIAPER

Marion Donovan's problem was one shared by every other young
housewife in New York in 1950. It was the middle of the baby
boom, and all those booming babies had leaky diapers. They also

had diapers that had to be washed, bleached, hung to dry, or laundered by an expensive diaper service. It's no surprise that Marion Donovan wished for a diaper that could simply be thrown away.

What is surprising, in this day of Pampers and Huggies and Luvs, is that no one seemed to agree with her. When Donovan created (out of a shower curtain and absorbent padding) the Boater in 1951, manufacturers turned down the product, saying it would be too expensive to produce.

Donovan's solution was to finance the manufacture of the Boater herself. Soon major department stores were carrying the snap-on, throwaway baby diaper, and Mrs. Donovan (along with a lot of babies) became extremely comfortable. Donovan eventually sold her firm (long before disposable diapers became a supermarket staple) for $1 million and went on to invent a skirt hanger that holds up to thirty items, and an elasticized zipper pull.

Ann Moore / *Andrea H. Proudfoot*

BABY CARRIERS

When Ann Moore served in the Peace Corps in the early 1960s, she spent most of her time with the natives of Togo in the former French West Africa. After returning to Colorado in 1964 and having her first child, she wished that the American culture offered a device like the African tribal baby carriers, which allowed women to bring their children along for the workday and promoted a close parent-child bonding as well.

Ann took a long piece of fabric and used it to attach daughter Mande to her chest, but the contrivance was awkward and Mande kept slipping off. Eventually, with the help of Mande's grandmother, Lucy Aukerman, Ann made a pouch from an old sheet, with straps that crisscrossed the back and with openings for the baby's hands and feet. Thanks to the child carrier, Ann could take Mande along with her wherever she went.

As more people saw Mande in her clever holder, they asked Ann where they could find a similar baby pouch. Through word of mouth and an ad in a mail-order catalogue, Moore and Aukerman found themselves with a prospering business, manufacturing the Snugli baby carrier.

In 1977 Ann Moore patented the Snugli, and she and her husband, Mike, started Snugli, Inc. By 1983 the firm was grossing $6 million a year. And Ann Moore—now over fifty and the mother of three grown children—feels she has contributed to the well-being of mothers and babies everywhere. "If the future holds a world of more loving adults," she said in 1984, "that's exciting."

One mother who was not happy with the Snugli baby carrier, however, was Andrea H. Proudfoot, of Eugene, Oregon. She received one as a gift and found it uncomfortable. She decided to design a baby carrier that took the weight of the child on the back rather than on the chest. "Andrea's Baby Pack" was patented, and Proudfoot employs fifteen women to sew the backpack and her other clothing designs in a small, cottage-industry firm.

Although Proudfoot has received buy-out offers from large corporations, she has held on to her patent rights for the Baby Pack and estimates that she nets $1,000 a month in income from her product.

Jane Wells

THE BABY JUMPER

In 1872 Mrs. Jane Wells of Chicago, Illinois, patented the baby jumper, which has become a nursery standard alongside the crib, playpen, and high chair.

"This machine may be operated by an infant from the time it can sit erect until it walks," said Wells in her patent application, "giving it the ability to dance, swing, and turn itself in any direction, affording it healthy and safe amusement, and relieving parents and nurses from much care and labor." Hardly changed in more than a century, the baby jumper still is giving a much-needed break to parents; the nurses are busy studying for their M.D.'s.

Wells's original model was made and marketed by the Occidental Manufacturing Company, where Jane's husband, Joel, worked as factory manager. Most of the assembly work at Occidental was performed by women, affording to them an employment opportunity rare in its day.

Gertrude Muller

T O I D Y

Mothers don't refer to a child's minitoilet seat as a "toidy" simply to mimic childlike pronunciation or out of embarrassment over the proper term. Rather, "Toidy Seat" is the brand name of the scaled-down toilet invented, manufactured, and marketed by Gertrude Agnes Muller; it has since entered the colloquial language, like Kleenex or Scrabble.

Gertrude Muller made a career of designing child-care products, including the safety auto seat and the folding booster seat. Born into a socially prominent Indiana family in 1887, the inventor herself neither married nor had children. The original idea for the toidy came to Gertrude around 1915, when her sister and a young niece were visiting. Gertrude was a secretary in a plumbing firm, and her sister wondered if they might find a way to get the company to build a better portable toilet for the child, as the existing product was large, clumsy, heavy, and inconvenient. They could and did. Gertrude designed it, her niece tested it, and the plumbing concern made it.

By 1924 Muller had established her own firm to market the toidy and attendant products: The Juvenile Wood Products Company. In later years (after the advent of plastics) it was renamed, simply, the Toidy Company. It remained a successful, family-owned firm through 1957, when Gertrude, the longtime company president, died of cancer at age sixty-seven.

Fannie Farmer

SCIENTIFIC RECIPES

It's not exactly something you can go down to the patent office and take out a number for, but Fannie Merritt Farmer did invent the recipe as we know it. Until the late 1880s, cooking instructions were always given by the "pinch," the "handful," or the "heaping spoon." It was the shy, red-haired Fannie Farmer whose *Boston Cooking School Cook Book* first introduced generations of aspiring homemakers to "one cup, sifted."

Fannie Farmer was born on March 23, 1857, in Boston, the city where she lived most of her life. At age sixteen she suffered a paralysis of the left leg, caused either by a mild stroke or a case of polio, and was left limping and unmarriageable by the standards of the day.

Fannie became a "mother's helper" in the household of a family friend, Mrs. Charles Shaw. It was there that Fannie learned to be a good cook and first conceived the idea of accurate recipes. Her charge, little Marcia, was puzzled by the directions for food preparations, and it was difficult to provide clear explanations for vague instructions. Fannie began to compile her own recipes in a standardized manner, if only to allow Marcia to duplicate them herself.

At age twenty-eight, seeking independence, Fannie enrolled in the Boston Cooking School and found her calling. By 1894 she was the school's assistant principal.

Although Farmer's greatest interest was in nutrition for hospital patients and the convalescent (she is credited with aiding Dr. Elliott P. Joslin in his research on diabetes), she is best known for the everyday recipes in her 1896 cookbook. When she first brought her manuscript to the publisher, however, the powers that be were so unsure of her newfangled "scientific" recipes that they insisted she pay production costs for the book herself. The volume went on to sell four million copies.

Miss Farmer continued to write and lecture until the First World War. Her monthly column in *The Women's Home Companion* survived for a decade. Despite two strokes later in life—which confined her to a wheelchair—Farmer continued to promote the cause of nutritionally sound food preparation.

Fannie Merritt Farmer died at age fifty-seven in her native Boston. "Miss Farmer's School of Cookery" outlived its founder by thirty years, finally closing in 1944.

Margaret Knight

BROWN PAPER BAGS

Margaret Knight's best-known invention is the brown paper bag—or, rather, the machinery that made the flat-bottomed sack possible. But this New England tomboy had patented twenty-seven inventions in her life (and constructed a few that were never patented), almost all in the field of heavy machinery.

Born in 1838, Mattie, as she was called, came up with her first viable invention when she was twelve years old. Her family was living in New Hampshire, and Mattie's older brother was working in the local textile mill. Visiting the factory one day, Mattie saw a worker injured when a shuttle slid out of its loom, piercing the man with its steel tip. On the spot, Mattie designed a stop-motion device that would prevent further such accidents. Although widely used, the device was never patented.

Knight's 1870 patent for the paper-bag–making machine was a successful one, refined and updated over the years and still in use today. Shortly after it was patented, she was offered—and refused—$50,000 for her rights. In the years between 1883 and 1894, she obtained a dozen more patents, for items ranging from window sashes to shoe-cutting devices. After the turn of the century, Mattie turned to the burgeoning field of automotive engineering, patenting valves, rotors, and engines. Most of the patents she assigned to her employers for spot cash, rather than collecting royalties over the years. Knight died in 1914, leaving a personal estate of only $275.05.

Lydia E. Pinkham

PATENT MEDICINE

The queen of patent medicine never actually patented a medicine. "Lydia E. Pinkham's Vegetable Compound" was a registered trademark, and the Pinkham family also registered with the U.S. Patent Office a logo that featured the benign, smiling countenance of grandmotherly Lydia herself. But the formula that was contained in the bottles was a standard home remedy of curative herbs, one that Lydia Pinkham had been using on her own children for years.

Composed of unicorn root, fenugreek, pleurisy root, black cohosh, and other botanicals preserved in 19 percent alcohol, Lydia Pinkham's patent medicine probably served more to create a mild euphoria in its consumers than to provide any real cure for "female complaints." It was, however, a less harmful remedy than the prescribed medical treatments of the day, which included nitric acid douches and "ovariectomies." Lydia E. Pinkham became a household name, and her advertising pamphlets became one of the few widespread disseminations on women's health and hygiene available to the American people.

Lydia Estes was born on February 9, 1819, one of twelve children in a liberal Quaker family from Massachusetts. Outspoken abolitionists and supporters of women's rights, the Estes family was often ostracized in its hometown. Lydia—five-foot-ten, with auburn hair and dark eyes—was both striking and fiercely independent. She worked as a schoolteacher, and surprised her friends and family when she married Isaac Pinkham in 1843. A widower of small means and intellect, Isaac was shorter than Lydia, somewhat chubby, and far less self-sufficient. By 1873 Lydia was mother to four children and nursemaid to her bankrupt, semi-invalid husband.

It was Lydia's middle son, Dan, who first thought to sell mom's homebrewed medicine for grocery money. For years neighbors and even strangers from other towns would come to the Pinkham household and stock up on her remedy. "Why can't we go into the business of making it and selling it, same as any other medicine?" queried Dan. At the time, there was no Food and Drug Administration to stop them; all one had to do to sell a cure-all to the public was advertise and distribute it. Popular home remedies included opium syrup and mercury ointment; Lydia E. Pinkham's Vegetable Compound was certainly no worse.

At first, the compound was marketed by the Pinkham children alone, who would distribute advertising flyers by bicycle and on foot. In 1876 the fledgling firm began advertising in the *Boston Herald* and shortly became a flourishing mail-order concern. With the addition of Lydia's picture to the product label in 1879, Lydia E. Pinkham's Vegetable Compound became a hit, and thousands of women turned to the real Lydia for medical advice.

Lydia herself wrote the sometimes informative, always exaggerated advertising copy for her product, and she distributed frank brochures about premenstrual syndrome, uterine collapse, and menopause with each bottle. Her compound would, according to its ads, make "the roses return to your cheeks, sallow looks depart, spirits brighten, your step become firm, and back and head aches be known no more." Customer endorsements (generally made up wholesale) credited the formula with shrinking tumors, replacing operations, alleviating insomnia, promoting appetite, and putting zip back into a lackluster marriage.

A "department of advice," which Lydia supervised, was staffed by women who would write personal answers to query letters received from customers. Many observers—including *The Ladies' Home Journal* and the U.S. government—would later claim that Lydia's soothing assurances often prevented women from seeking proper medical care. It is also true, however, that when Lydia began encouraging simple measures like cleanliness and exercise, the established medical community was encouraging operations that offered a 40 percent mortality rate.

Lydia's business-minded sons both died of tuberculosis in 1881; Lydia suffered a stroke in early 1883 and died five months later. Her descendants feuded bitterly over control of the firm. Keeping alive the tradition of Lydia's advice department even after Lydia's death, one Pinkham heir urged consumers to "write to Mrs. Pinkham"—and gave the letters to his wife to answer. A photograph of Lydia's grave, published in *The Ladies' Home Journal* in 1905 as part of a campaign against proprietary medicines, created an international scandal when it proved without a doubt that the *real* Mrs Pinkham, having been dead for some twenty-two years, couldn't have been writing those friendly notes.

Despite bad publicity, Lydia Pinkham's patent medicine company became a $3-million-a-year business by the 1920s; it was passed down in the family through 1968, when the product was absorbed by Cooper Laboratories, and was still manufactured and marketed well into the 1970s. Lydia Pinkham herself never grew rich from the multimillion-dollar enterprise she founded; the first dividend on Pinkham stock was paid in 1885, two years after her death. But she did become the most familiar female face in America at one time, and, in an era that equated weakness and sickliness with femininity, she was a visible and valuable spokeswoman for health.

Designing Women

THE FIELD OF DESIGN encompasses everything from personal vanity to commercial decor; "designing women" includes the first Egyptian who smeared her eyelids with kohl, to the lighting engineers of the twentieth century who combined technology with art.

Design boasts physiological advances like Anna Kalso's negative-heel shoe, and constructs like the store mannequin—invented by a Madame Paquin and first displayed in 1900 in Paris. The great cosmeticians were inventors, entrepreneurs, and showwomen combined; the arbiters of fashion invented their styles.

The bra, unsurprisingly, could command a chapter all on its own. Although one Otto Titzling claims credit for the invention, the pun-making possibilities of his name seem to have done more for his reputation than any documentary evidence (he never took out a patent). The same goes for the flamboyant charlatan of the Roaring Twenties, Philippe de Brassière. Yet Olga Erteszek alone holds twenty-eight bra patents—they are the, ah, foundation of her Olga Corporation—and patents are held as well by original designer Polly Jacob (a.k.a. Caresse Crosby) and innovator Ida ("Maidenform") Rosenthal.

Caresse Crosby / Ida Cohen Rosenthal

THE BRASSIERE

"When I made my debut," recalled Caresse Crosby in her auto-biography *The Passionate Years* (Dial Press, 1953), "girlish figures were being encased in a sort of boxlike armor of whalebone and pink cordage. This contraption ran upwards from the knee to under the armpit. Over the top of it was firmly hooked a corset-cover of muslin or silk. . . . If petting had been practiced in those days, it could never have gone very far."

Although she would later make a reputation as a sexually liberated woman (shockingly so), Caresse Crosby—at this time still known as Polly Jacob—did not invent the brassiere in order to promote a sample of what would become her chosen name. Rather, her bulky corset cover one pre–World War I evening was showing over her décolletage as well as hampering her freedom of movement. She demanded two silk handkerchiefs, a length of pink ribbon, and a needle and thread from her lady's maid, Marie, and constructed the first modern bra on the spot. It was not one of the lifting-and-shaping contrivances that would later be designed by Ida Rosenthal or Olga Erteszek, but rather a way to squash the bustline quite flat against the chest, as was considered proper for an unmarried lady of the day.

The "backless brassiere," as Polly called it, was a blessed relief from her confining undergarments. She showed it to her girl-friends in secret, and most of them begged Marie to sew them something similar. "It was only when a stranger from Boston wrote enclosing a dollar . . . that I decided I had something to exploit," Polly recalled. (Otto Titzling, who claimed to have invented the brassiere in 1912, never patented it. Philippe de Brassière claimed to have invented it and named it after himself as late as 1929, a ploy refuted in court. The word "brassiere" is actually derived from the Old French for "upper arm.")

That teenaged Mary Phelps "Polly" Jacob would actually consider earning money from an invention was an indication of how different she was from her peers. She was born into the Social Register and absolute privilege; "trade" was to be scorned. Her great-great-great-great grandfather, after all, came over on the *Mayflower*. She called J. P. Morgan "Uncle Jack." Lady Baden-Powell named her the first official Girl Scout in America. Why would this rarefied creature want to operate a sweatshop? Yet, she did.

However, for the spoiled children of the upper crust, pocket money—while too crude to request—was too precious to ignore. Polly hired a patent lawyer (on credit) and set about securing rights to the "backless brassiere." A U.S. patent was granted in 1914. The inventor then borrowed $100, rented two sewing machines, and hired two immigrant girls to sew bras in a "secret sweatshop," as she called it. Hundreds of bras were manufactured, and Polly took them personally to the finer stores of New York. The reception was noticeably cool.

So when, a few years later—long after her childlike whim of becoming a textile tycoon had faded—a family friend offered to negotiate a sale of the patent to the Warner Brothers Corset Company, Polly agreed. When she was offered $1,500 for all rights, she thought it "not only adequate, but magnificent." By Polly's best estimate, Warner made $15 million from the invention over the next three decades.

Still, disappointment over the "Jacob Brassiere Co.," or whatever she planned to call it, hardly shadowed Polly's life. Her debut season was just a taste of what was to come. She married her childhood sweetheart, Dick Peabody (of the Peabody Museum Peabodys) in 1915, shortly before he left to fight in the First World War. She bore two children, William and Polleen, and lived in relative luxury. In 1921 she met charismatic banker/poet Harry Crosby—he a bachelor of twenty-one, she a married woman of twenty-seven. After a short battle with her conscience, she divorced Dick and ran off to Paris with Harry in what was one of the great scandals of its day.

"Life with Harry was a hedonistic adventure," she wrote. Life with Harry was an eye-popper. By 1927 Harry Crosby had quit his bank job (with "Uncle Jack's" Paris branch) to devote himself to poetry; Mary Crosby changed her name to Caresse and did likewise. Caresse rode naked on a baby elephant down the Champs-Élysées to herald an art students' ball. Harry bought an antique rural mill for the couple by writing a check on his wife's sleeve for whatever amount was in his bank account—and he had absolutely no idea how much was in the account. The pair traveled to Egypt, Syria, and Palestine; they dabbled with opium, sun worship, and orgies. They never received guests but from their huge bed, and they often invited callers to bathe with them in a Roman tub.

In 1927 the pair founded Black Sun Press, which released beautiful limited editions by James Joyce, D. H. Lawrence, Hart Crane, and Ezra Pound. Although the firm was originally a vanity press for their own work, the Crosbys found themselves introducing many important writing talents to Europe or back in America.

Traveling around Europe on fabulous flights of fancy throughout the 1920s, the Crosbys were a storybook couple whose tale had a tragic ending. Caresse was shattered when Harry Crosby took his own life in December 1929. Back in the United States by the start of World War II, Caresse lowered her profile considerably—but not her love of flamboyance, art, and, especially, invention.

In the early 1930s, Caresse tried to interest New York publishers in the idea of releasing low-cost, paperback editions of Black

Sun books—or any books, for that matter. Such paperbound volumes "sold in their respective countries for the equivalent of 25 cents to 50 cents," Caresse said, "and by their enormous circulation proved to me that more people would read more if books cost less." Random House, Simon & Schuster, and Doubleday all disagreed.

"I'm also descended from Robert Fulton, the inventor of the steamboat," Caresse once noted. "I believe that my ardor for invention springs from his loins. I can't say that the brassiere will ever take as great a place in history as the steamboat, but I did invent it. And perpetual motion has always been just around the corner."

Caresse Crosby's "backless brassiere" was made obsolete in the 1920s, thanks to an invention by Ida Cohen Rosenthal, a pint-sized Jewish émigré from Russia. The Rosenthal brassiere was the first to use cups to support the breasts and the first to come in a variety of sizes. Initially used as a sales gimmick for Ida's dressmaking business—she gave them away, because they made her dresses look better—the bras became the basis of the multimillion-dollar Maidenform company.

Ida Kaganovich was born in 1886 near Minsk and fled the Tsarist regime for America in 1904, where the family name was changed to Cohen. Ida set herself up as a seamstress in a small shop in Hoboken, New Jersey, and married William Rosenthal in 1906, who helped her with the shop.

The First World War created a market for ready-to-wear clothing, and the Rosenthal business grew from one hired hand in the living room to twenty employees in Manhattan premises. In the early 1920s, Ida bought a half interest in a fashionable dress shop on East Fifty-seventh Street, and it was there that she first designed the bra as we know it.

The boyish flapper dresses of the day looked fine with the Crosby model of flat-fronted brassieres—provided the wearer had a rail-slim figure. Fuller-figured women looked much better with a little more support, and Ida designed a garment with a few strategic tucks and a couple of snaps in the back that would allow the

This turn-of-the-century photographers' model was highly sought after for her wasplike waist—a perfect advertisement for corset makers. Unfortunately, the petite waistline was actually the result of increasingly tightened bindings, and the woman finally died of asphyxiation. Undergarment rebels like Caresse Crosby and Ida Rosenthal put an end to this self-torture.

59

shifts to fall in a more flattering manner. The bras were given away to promote dress sales, but soon customers were returning to buy the bras alone. Ida and William Rosenthal scraped together $4,500 and incorporated the Maiden Form Brassiere Company in 1923. By 1938 the firm had a gross annual income of $4.5 million—and would reach $40 million annually in the 1960s.

William Rosenthal, an amateur sculptor who had experience in ready-to-wear clothing manufacture, was head of production for the company. It was he who came up with the precursor to the A, B, C, and D sizings that have become industry standards. Ida was in charge of everything else: treasurer, sales manager, advertising director. The company's methods of mass production were innovative, as was their incentive program for employees.

Ida Rosenthal stood four feet, eleven inches tall, a vivacious, petite whirlwind of activity. (She is said to have ordered male business associates to sit down in her presence so that they wouldn't tower over her.) Ida traveled around the world drumming up business for the firm, which eventually boasted sales in more than a hundred countries and manufacturing facilities in England, Canada, Puerto Rico, and Trinidad. Ida continued to travel the world representing her firm until well into her eighties. She was widowed in 1958 and became president of the company, then called Maidenform, Inc.

A noted philanthropist and ambassador of goodwill worldwide, Ida Rosenthal died of pneumonia in 1973 at the age of eighty-seven half a century after changing—literally—the profile of American women. She handed the reins of Maidenform to her daughter, Beatrice Coleman.

Harriet Hubbard Ayer / Helena Rubinstein / Elizabeth Arden

COSMETICS

Until the turn of the century, makeup was something no respectable woman would consider applying to her face. "Painted lady" was synonymous with streetwalker. At the same time, however, women were allowed—even encouraged—to have a myriad of mysterious "women's ailments," and over-the-counter medications did land-office business. It's not surprising, then, that cosmetics came to be acceptable by virtue of being first disguised as cures. The face creams for sunburn, blemishes, and freckles that innovative cosmeticians put on the market slowly found themselves becoming inbued with flattering color. Mascara was not far behind. In forty years, cosmetics went from being no industry at all to becoming one of the twenty largest industries in the country. By the 1960s, it would be in the top ten.

Three flamboyant women, working separately and sometimes in heated competition, virtually created this massive consumer industry from scratch. While none was an inventor in the hands-on sense, each masterminded the creation of her formulas: identifying the need, conceiving the product, and overseeing its manufacture. Just as Coco Chanel sniffed bottles of perfume No. 5 (her lucky number, not her fifth effort) until it met her ideal, the *grandes dames* of early American cosmetology bought, begged, or borrowed the right idea at the right time to build their empires.

The earliest of these cosmetics pioneers started with the greatest advantages in life and ended with the fewest. Harriet Hubbard was born in 1849 (or thereabouts; international beauties often are unreliable in reporting their ages) to a prosperous family in Chicago. She was well educated but, surprisingly, a painfully shy child who thought of herself as an ugly duckling. Harriet married Herbert Copeland Ayer in 1865.

As the pampered mother of two (a third child had died in infancy; another would later die in the Chicago Fire), Harriet Hubbard Ayer began to blossom. She traveled, read, studied French poetry, entertained actors and artists in her home, and gained a reputation as a great beauty. It was, in fact, because of her increasing independence and self-esteem that she was divorced from Mr. Ayer in 1886.

Harriet moved to New York City, where she was viewed as a great lady fallen upon evil times. She became a saleslady at a fancy furniture store but looked for a business venture she could operate on her own. It was the chemist who concocted her personal fragrance that led her to her fortune: M. Mirault told her of a face cream that his grandfather had prepared for the legendary Mme. Récamier, a siren from the court of Napoleon, that allegedly kept her skin as youthful as a girl's. Harriet immediately bought the formula and, backed with borrowed money, started a business manufacturing and distributing it.

Harriet Hubbard Ayer created quite a scandal when she put her own name on her beauty cream (along with her family coat of arms). In 1886 the only time a "proper" lady expected to have her name in print was in her birth announcement, marriage banns, and obituary. Scandal brought success; Lily Langtry endorsed Recamier Preparations, and society women flocked to Mrs. Ayer's shop.

The success of her firm was short-lived, however. Harriet was sued by her financial backer and her own daughter (who was also the backer's daughter-in-law), charged with mismanaging family finances; she countercharged that her family was plotting to drive her insane. In 1893 her ex-husband and her daughter committed Harriet to a mental institution, where she remained for fourteen miserable months. The cosmetics company was sold, and with it rights to the Harriet Hubbard Ayer name.

The end of Mrs. Ayer's life took a positive swing, however. Thanks in part to her public activity on the part of fellow ill-treated mental patients, Harriet felt equipped to apply for a job as a columnist at the *New York World* in 1886. She became an institution of the Sunday supplement, the first coordinator of a "woman's page." Two books of her advice were published in hardcover. She also began to invent beauty formulas of her own in this period, creating an antiperspirant, a hair straightener, and a variety of cold creams. She never patented any of her own formulas, however, and reportedly gave them away instead of selling them.

Harriet Hubbard Ayer died of pneumonia in 1903, having made the first step to legitimization of costmetics. Soon afterward, two other women would build fortunes on her foundation.

Helena Rubinstein was born in approximately 1870 in Cracow, Poland. As she related the story, her parents were well-to-do and she studied medicine briefly in Zurich, Switzerland, before immigrating to Australia in the wake of an unhappy love affair. Packed in her trunk, she wrote, were twelve jars of beauty cream developed by a Hungarian chemist for Helena's mother.

A more probable version of history has it that Helena came from a poor family in the Jewish ghetto, worked as a waitress and in other unglamorous positions, and sailed to Australia to seek a better life. Either way, she did establish a successful business near Melbourne, selling her "creme valaz" as a salve for sunburned Australian complexions. By 1908 she had saved $100,000 in profits and moved her shop to London.

Miss Rubinstein (or Madame Rubinstein, as she styled herself) married an American newspaperman, Edward Titus, and opened the first beauty salon in England. The couple had two children, opened a salon in Paris, and moved to America before the advent of World War I. Rubinstein's Maison de Beauté on Forty-ninth Street in Manhattan became the hub of a nationwide chain of salons—and the focal point of an intense rivalry between Rubinstein and Elizabeth Arden, whose signature salon was located nearby on Fifth Avenue.

The culture shock of the war created a vastly expanded market for Rubinstein products; it also began the rift that separated her from her husband. Edward Titus left for France in 1916 and joined the underground literary set. Although Titus's Black Mannequin Press was publishing work by up-and-coming authors such as D. H. Lawrence, James Joyce, and Ernest Hemingway, Mme. Rubinstein saw no profit in it and cut off her husband's funds.

Financial acuity—even to the point of tightfistedness—always was a Rubinstein trademark. Her great fortune was made from the great stock market crash of 1929. In 1928 Mme. Rubinstein sold her entire enterprise for $3 million. A year later, she bought it back for $1.5 million. Few Wall Street brokers were pleased with the masterstroke of this four-foot, ten-inch foreigner, who still peppered her conversation with Yiddish phrases. (A typical Rubinstein business transaction: When told she couldn't rent the penthouse apartment in a chic Park Avenue complex because no Jews were allowed, she bought the building.)

Mme. Rubinstein promoted the healing properties of her creams and lotions and continued to turn her nose up fashionably at their "painting" properties throughout the 1920s. "I do not object to a little rouge and to a discriminating use of powder," she said. "But some of the creams which so many girls and women apply as a base on which to put on an elaborate makeup are ruinous to the natural beauty of the complexion." Helena traveled to Africa, India, and the Orient to research cosmetics art, handing over plenty of Western coin to learn their secrets. As far as she was concerned, the only reason why women didn't spend time improving their appearances was "due to one of three things: ignorance, laziness, or a happy marriage."

Rubinstein was no chemist, but she did oversee the development of the first waterproof mascara and a line of medicated face creams. She made money in every area in which she ventured, and she kept her business interests strictly in the family. In 1938 she legally divorced Titus (after a separation of twenty years) and married Artchil Gourielli-Tchkonia, a prince from Russian Georgia. He was twenty years her junior, yet Helena outlived him. Prince Artchil died in 1956; Mme. Rubinstein lived until 1965, never having stopped working. In her nineties, she would conduct business from her bed. Her estate was valued at more than $130 million—

$500,000 of which went to build the Helena Rubinstein Pavilion art museum in Tel Aviv.

Rivaling Rubinstein at every turn was Elizabeth Arden, a woman equally as driven and equally as innovative. The two expanded their business competition into a fierce personal battle. Once, Arden raided the Rubinstein staff, hiring away eleven of her best personnel. Rubinstein retaliated by hiring Arden's ex-husband. Rubinstein married a prince in 1938; Arden married a prince in 1942. Arden traveled the world visiting beauty salons yet refused to set foot in the shop of "that woman," as she called Rubinstein. The press, of course, ate it up.

Elizabeth Arden was born Florence Nightingale Graham to a family of tenant farmers living near Toronto, Canada. She took the name Elizabeth Arden only when she opened her first salon: The "Elizabeth" was already engraved on the gilt nameplate, and Florence happened to be reading Tennyson's *Enoch Arden* at the time. So she had the signmaker add "Arden" to the existing plaque rather than spend extra money on having the whole thing redone.

Graham never finished high school; she escaped crushing poverty by fleeing to New York after an unsuccessful stab at career life with stints as a dental assistant, a cashier, and a stenographer. Florence was thirty years old and had little to show for it except a naturally lustrous complexion. Her face became the key to her fortune.

By 1908 women were allowing themselves to aid nature with the odd lotion and cream. Everyone wanted skin like Florence Graham's, and when she took a job as a facial masseuse in a New York beauty shop, she was her own best advertisement.

With a small loan from her brother, Florence opened her first salon on Fifth Avenue—the one whose nameplate gave her company its name. (In fact, Florence never did have her name legally changed.) She gradually modified her face creams into makeup foundations, and her salons flourished nationwide. She helped formulate the first nongreasy skin cream, Amoretta, and introduced lipstick shades coordinated to skin tone and clothing. By the 1920s, Elizabeth Arden boasted more than a hundred salon locations.

In 1915 Graham/Arden married Thomas Lewis Jenkins, a bank officer whom she had met while applying for a loan. He continued to work for her after their 1934 divorce; it took Helena Rubinstein herself to sever their business relationship. In 1942 Arden married Prince Michael Evalanoff, cementing her position in high society.

Elizabeth Arden was a masterful woman who disguised her strength in pink dresses. She owned the Elizabeth Arden company lock, stock, and barrel, and pushed it to reach $60 million in annual sales. She also made a fortune in horse racing: In 1947 her Jet Pilot won the Kentucky Derby. She traveled around the world, threw elaborate charity balls, and sold her firm to Eli Lilly and Company rather than let it outlive her. Florence Graham died at the age of eighty-eight (by her calculations; she may have been closer to ninety-three) with the grim satisfaction of having outlived her archrival Helena Rubinstein by eighteen months.

Julie Newmar

''CHEEKY DERRIÈRE'' PANTYHOSE

Actress/dancer Julie Newmar, whose legs were once insured for a million dollars, is eminently qualified to design and patent a new type of pantyhose. She calls her invention "body perfecting hose" but the U.S. Patent Office decided that "cheeky derrière" was more accurate. (See Foreword for her account of this encounter.) In any case, the hose are constructed to push up the buttocks, giving the wearer "a more natural appearance."

"The trouble with the current design of pantyhose is that they flatten your behind. It looks very artificial," she says. She solved the problem by cutting the panty hose on the bias, diagonal to the grain of the fabric, and elasticizing the center seam.

The tall (five-foot, eleven-inch), strawberry-blond star of stage, film, and television only looks—and, some might say, sounds—Scandinavian. She was actually born in Los Angeles in 1935 to an engineering professor and a veteran showgirl from the Ziegfeld Follies. By age seven, Julie had already seen the bright lights. "I was 'encouraged' to perform for two matinees, as 'Alice in Wonderland.' Eight years of unemployment followed," she quips.

After a stint as a choreographer/dance instructor/double for Universal Studios, she began blazing a name for herself. In her first dramatic role on Broadway, opposite Charles Boyer in *The Marriage-Go-Round,* she won a Tony award. She would go on to capture rolls in six other Broadway musicals, including *Guys and Dolls, Li'l Abner,* and *Dames at Sea.*

Miss Newmar entered the national scene in the film version of *The Marriage-Go-Round,* in which she reprised her role of a Scandinavian superwoman trying to steal Susan Hayward's husband. She had roles in five other feature films, notably as "one fourteenth" of *Seven Brides for Seven Brothers* and recently (1985) in *Streetwalkin'.*

She is most famous, though, for her starring roles in two of the sixties' campiest TV series: Rhoda the Robot in *My Living Doll* and the Catwoman in *Batman.* The latter is still in syndication. She has also guest-starred in fifty other TV shows, and fondly remembers committing suicide in *Columbo.*

While at home she is most likely to be dressed in leotards, lately she has been resorting to a business suit for her new career as a real estate developer. She personally designed and oversaw the construction of a shopping center near Beverly Hills. As for the "body perfecting hose"—it has yet to be manufactured, but she still has hope. "A leading French firm is now interested in the patent, but who knows if anything will come of it? It can be very frustrating to have an invention that's ahead of its time. But then again, Leonardo da Vinci had to wait four hundred years for his to fly!"

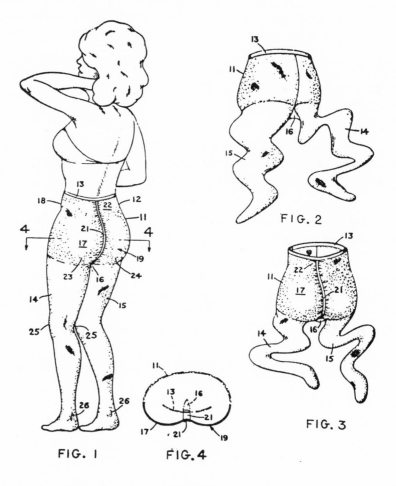

These simple drawings of a unique idea were sufficient to earn actress Julie Newmar patent #3,914,799 for "Cheeky Derrière Relief" in 1975.

Sarah Breedlove Walker

HAIR STRAIGHTENER

Sarah Breedlove Walker, a widowed black washerwoman, invented her method for straightening Afro-American hair "in a dream" in 1905, and mixed up her pomades and ointments in washtubs. A decade later, Mme. C. J. Walker, as she became known, was the wealthiest black woman in America, and the Walker Method of hair care employed three thousand sales agents around the country and was widely copied in the United States and Europe.

Sarah Breedlove was born in 1867 on the Louisiana Delta to a farming family, orphaned in childhood, and married at age fourteen. By age twenty she was a widow, moving to St. Louis to support herself and her daughter A'Lelia by taking in laundry.

It was there that Sarah invented the hairdressing techniques that would unkink hair so that black women could assimilate the white fashions of the day. She manufactured her hair-growing pomade, soaps, and shampoos in the kitchen, and had some success selling the products in her neighborhood. Soon she moved to Denver, Colorado, to join her brother, and there met and married Charles J. Walker, a newspaperman.

Mrs. Walker not only invented her line of products but also established the sales technique that firms like Avon have since utilized so effectively. Starting out selling her products door-to-door, she soon recruited a sales force of "beauty culturists" who, dressed uniformly in a starched, spotless white shirt and long black skirt, would take the Walker products to homes all over the country.

69

Mrs. Walker set up a manufacturing plant in Denver and another one in Pittsburgh. In 1910 she moved the company's headquarters to Indianapolis.

Mme. Walker was a vigorous self-promoter, putting her portrait on her packaging and giving lecture tours and demonstrations around the United States. She personally trained all Walker agents, and the Mme. C. J. Walker Manufacturing Company—of which she was president and sole owner—became one of the biggest employers of black women in the country, giving work to three thousand sales agents in the United States and the Caribbean. Except for the superstars of the stage, Mme. Walker was the most famous woman of her race; she amassed a fortune of more than $1 million.

Mrs. Walker gave generously to the National Association for the Advancement of Colored People (NAACP) and established scholarships at Tuskegee Institute. Her employees formed "Walker Clubs" to promote community service. A'Lelia became a patroness of the arts—her intellectual salon was called the "Dark Tower"—and Sarah commissioned black architect Vertner Tandy to build a $250,000 mansion for mother and daughter.

Mme. Walker died on May 25, 1919, while her empire was at its height. Diagnosed as suffering from kidney disease, she had nonetheless refused to slow down. She left her business to A'Lelia, and a huge trust fund for Negro orphanages, old-age homes, and schools.

Ellen Demorest / *Eleanor Butterick*

PAPER DRESS PATTERNS

The ubiquitous paper dress pattern was patented by and is generally credited to the husband-and-wife team of Ebenezer and Eleanor Butterick of Massachusetts. Rights were preserved in Ebenezer's name in 1863. However, it was another husband-and-wife team, William and Ellen Demorest, who first exploited the idea of sew-at-home guides for fashionable garments, and although their idea has not preserved their logo—as it did for the competition—the invention did make them rich and powerful in their own time.

Ellen "Nell" Demorest first began marketing dress patterns in 1860 after watching her maid cut sewing guides from wrapping paper. Using disposable cutouts to help fit clothing was not a new idea; selling paper duplicates of current fashion for do-it-yourselfers with sewing machines (a recent invention itself) was. Nell and William devised a system of sizing tissue-paper dress components and, within five years, had a network of three hundred distributors nationwide. Their monthly pattern book, *Mme. Demorest's Mirror of Fashion,* had a circulation of sixty thousand, and the Demorests' social lives were reported by *The New York Times.*

Ellen Louise Curtis was born in 1824 to a successful millinery family. When she was eighteen and finished with school, her father set Ellen up in the hat trade in Troy, New York, but she soon relocated to the more competitive environment of New York City. There she met William Jennings Demorest, a widower with two children, and married him in 1858. She was, by then, a prosperous businesswoman in her own right, and even giving birth to a son in 1859 did not deter her from pursuing her career.

William Demorest fancied himself a bit of an inventor, and he held patents for sewing-machine attachments and accessories. His fortunes were at a low ebb when he married Nell, however, and he immediately latched on to paper dress patterns as a surefire get-rich-quick scheme. He was right.

The Demorests started packaging replicas of the latest styles in the flat envelopes so familiar today, and they illustrated the front flap with colored fashion plates. They printed a monthly woman's magazine to promote their mail-order sales and launched it to an immediate wide circulation by enclosing a free sample pattern in each issue. The magazine evolved into an outspoken advocate of women's rights, abolition, and temperance, which was hardly hypocritical on the part of its publishers. Not only did Mrs. (or Mme., as she preferred) Demorest assume a full administrative role in the company, but also the manufacturing branch of the firm was one of the few large employers in the country that hired blacks on equal terms with whites and that situated them side-by-side in the workplace. There were those who refused to buy Demorest patterns because they were made in an integrated shop.

"I do not claim that all women, or a large portion of them, should enter into independent business relations with the world," said Mme. Demorest at the 1876 Centennial Exposition. "But I do claim that all women should cultivate and respect in themselves an ability to make money as they respect in their fathers, husbands, and brothers the same ability."

The Demorests went on to patent other, less significant inventions: a combination suspender and shoulder brace; a scaled-down hoop skirt; and an "Imperial dress elevator," which raised and lowered one's skirts in the face of curbs and puddles. While these devices were all credited to Mme. Demorest, some biographers feel that these inventions were mainly William's ideas. Selling both these popular items and a high volume of patterns, the Demorest retail and mail-order empire continued to prosper throughout the 1870s. In 1876 alone, the firm sold three million paper patterns.

Soon, however, competition from the Buttericks began to overwhelm them. The Demorests tried to prove a priority claim for the pattern invention in court but failed, and the Buttericks kept exclusivity on the patent. William Demorest retired from the business in 1885; Nell retired in 1887, and the company was sold.

Tall, energetic Nell Demorest died of a cerebral hemorrhage in 1898 at age seventy-three, having survived her husband by three years. She left behind a fortune in cash and two service organizations: Sorosis, the influential women's organization that she co-founded; and the Welcome Lodging House, a refuge for abused women and children.

Elizabeth Miller

BLOOMERS

Bloomers were named after women's rights activist Amelia Bloomer, but she didn't invent them. This combination of thigh-length skirt and Turkish trousers (rather than the puffy underwear we associate with the term today) was designed by Elizabeth Smith Miller in 1851 as an alternative to impractical, floor-sweeping dresses.

Ironically one of the more conservative members of a family headed by philanthropist/reformer Gerrit Smith (an antislavery activist and role model for cousin Elizabeth Cady Stanton), Elizabeth Smith married prominent New York lawyer Charles Dudley Miller at age twenty-one. A reasonably contented homemaker, Elizabeth actually invented the bloomer for the acceptably feminine task of gardening. Annoyed by yards of material trapping her legs as she tried to weed and prune, she pieced together a work outfit of what she called "a short dress" combined with "Turkish trousers to the ankle." It was, she felt, an acceptable compromise between modesty and practicality.

When Mrs. Miller visited her suffragette cousin, both Mrs. Stanton and houseguest Amelia Bloomer were taken with this ingenious outfit. They began wearing the "pantalettes," as they called them, everywhere, and Bloomer wrote an article advocating their use in her feminist magazine *Lily*. Subscriptions to *Lily* doubled overnight; the editors were deluged with requests for a pattern.

Skirts reaching a mere four inches below the knee were scandalous in the 1850s; woman wearing what became known as the "Bloomer costume" were routinely chucked out of public places. By 1860 both Miller and Bloomer herself had given up the pantalettes—Bloomer because the furor drew attention away from the more basic issues of women's rights, and Miller because she was content with "the old swaddling clothes," as she put it. When she died in 1911 at age eighty-eight, Miller said she was less proud of her revolutionary clothing design than she was of the book she had written thirty years earlier: *In the Kitchen*.

Claire McCardell

LEOTARDS

When fashion designer Claire McCardell invented the stretch leotard in the 1940s (the leotard itself was invented by, and named for, nineteenth-century French acrobat Jules Leotard), her intention was to provide an extra layer of warmth for college girls living in dormitories left unheated because of wartime fuel shortages.

Most of McCardell's contributions to fashion were marked by their ingenuity and practicality as well as their popularity. She created the first "separates" so that working girls could mix and match a wardrobe on a limited budget. She invented the tent dress because it seemed a comfortable thing to wear herself. She popularized denim because it was inexpensive. And she pioneered the use of cotton fabric as an alternative to hard-to-handle satins and brocades.

Claire McCardell was born on May 24, 1905, in Frederick, Maryland, the eldest of four children and the only daughter of Adrian McCardell, president of the Frederick County Bank and a state senator. She was a restless student at Hood College when she transferred to the New York School of Fine and Applied Arts—now known as the Parsons School of Design. After graduation in 1928, Claire took a job painting rosebuds on lampshades while she perfected design skills in her spare time. In 1931, when Townley Frocks' staff designer died suddenly in the middle of the fashion season, design trainee McCardell got a chance to work on her own creations.

Although the garment industry was slowly giving in to the concept of "ready-to-wear," McCardell's revolutionary designs did not catch on quickly. Her 1938 groundbreaker, the tent dress (patterned after a Moroccan robe), was scorned by buyers when first shown. It literally hung in a corner of her office while she left town on vacation. In her absence, a Best & Co. buyer noticed the loose-fitting garment and ordered a hundred copies. Within a year, "the Monastic" was the rage of Seventh Avenue, and "the American Look" was launched.

World War II itself brought Claire McCardell into her own. Ground war in Europe reduced communication with—and the influence of—Parisian fashion arbiters. Shortages of labor and material made her practical innovations vital, and a growing class of women wage-earners provided a larger market for ready-to-wear. The McCardell "Popover," a denim wraparound housedress, made Claire literally a household name: It was intended as a work outfit for women whose servants had left for wartime factory jobs.

In 1950 McCardell became the first fashion designer voted annual "Women of Achievement" by the National Women's Press Club; she was on the cover of *Time* magazine in 1956. She had married architect Irving Harris in the last year of the war, and she became a partner in Townley Frocks in 1952. She was the first fashion designer to franchise her creations—jewelry, sweaters, raincoats, and granny sunglasses—and was working on a line of designer paper dolls when she died of cancer on March 22, 1958, at age fifty-two.

Mary Quant

MINISKIRT

When Mary Quant was presented with the Order of the British Empire in 1966 for her contribution to Britain's balance of trade, she wore a miniskirt to Buckingham Palace. It would have been a socially unacceptable gesture from anyone else but, after all, it was Quant's miniskirt that launched the "Carnaby Street look" and gave a much-needed boost to the English export market.

Mary Quant was born in London in 1934, and she attended Goldsmith College of Art after a scattered early education. When she opened the shop Bazaar in Chelsea in 1955, she and her husband-to-be, Alexander Plunket-Greene, would sew the next day's sales line overnight in their front parlor. Soon the couple was employing seamstresses and instituting mass-production methods that would turn their tiny boutique into a mini-empire. Quant and Plunket-Greene married in 1957, by which time their shop was selling about a hundred dresses a month. These late-1950s prototypes featured dangerously short skirts, but their use was largely confined to a subset of swinging Londoners. Things really started to take off for the couple—and the mini—when they held their first American show in 1965.

The miniskirt may have been a reinvention as much as an invention (look at the flapper dresses of the 1920s, for instance, which fell six and even nine inches above the knee), but Quant's entrepreneurial flair made it the signature of a decade. It was introduced to the market almost simultaneously in 1963 by French designer André Courrèges, but he is best remembered for his trademark boots; Quant took the heat for a garment that, as then-New York City Mayor John Lindsay quipped, "enables young ladies to run faster and, because of it, they may have to!"

Even after *Vogue* magazine proudly displayed the mini in its March 1964 issue—giving it the stamp of fashion approval—the knee-revealing item was still a topic of controversy. American high-school girls became used to a demeaning routine of kneeling before the school principal: Anyone whose skirt didn't then sweep the ground was dismissed from class for the day. When the micro-skirt—a skirt no larger than a wide belt—began edging into the market, "decent folk" were appalled. "A vestment of harlots," cried the administration of St. Hilda's College in Britain.

After 1970 a no-longer-rebellious Quant joined the "fashion establishment." The Quant lines were franchised by major retailers, such as J. C. Penney, and she expanded into cosmetics (distributed by Max Factor), hosiery, linens, dolls, and interior decorations. By the mid-1970s, the miniskirt debate had faded, and a new debate took its place. Women were starting to wear *trousers*. If the miniskirt was banned from church, the pantsuit was banned from public restaurants. Before the decade was over, women were—possibly for the first time in history—sole arbiters of their own hemlines.

Anna Kalso

EARTH SHOE

The negative-heel Earth Shoe became a signature of the 1970s, just as the miniskirt was of the 1960s. Hippies supplanted mods, and form began to follow function. Everybody was "laid-back"—even to their soles.

The orthopedic footwear design of Danish Yoga instructor Anna Kalso was named Earth Shoe because it made its U.S. debut on Earth Day, a 1970 celebration of the counterculture. However, Kalso had been wearing and making negative-heel shoes since the 1950s, when she saw the natural gait of barefooted primitive tribespeople whom she encountered on her world travels. In soft soil or sand, the heel leaves an impression lower than that of the toes; yet Westerners insist on building up the heels of their shoes. This was unnatural and threw off the entire carriage of the body, argued Kalso. Her shoes—clunky and even ugly-looking but very comfortable—were built so that the heel was cushioned at a level below that of the ball.

From a single store in Copenhagen, Kalso soon had branches throughout Europe and the United States. Although the Earth Shoe design fell from favor after the "me decade," the firm still manufactures the product. Anna Kalso left the shoe business when she turned seventy, but she continues to design "healthy" apparel in her retirement, which she divides between homes in Denmark and Arizona.

Loie Fuller / Mary E. H. Greenewalt / Jean Rosenthal

LIGHTING DESIGN

At a time when the role of women in the theater arts was confined largely to performing, Loie Fuller, Mary E. H. Greenewalt, and Jean Rosenthal pioneered the use of light and color. With their mechanical inventions and design innovations, they changed forever the way we, the audience, see.

Although they probably never met, their achievements in lighting design paralleled and overlapped each other's, which is ironic because each approached her work from a dramatically different angle: Fuller, the emotional, exotic dancer in pursuit of art; Greenewalt, the intellectual concert pianist in pursuit of theory; and Rosenthal, the no-nonsense professional in pursuit of the next deadline.

A reputation as a seminal lighting designer was not Loie Fuller's intention. By the time she began experimenting with incandescent bulbs and colors in 1891, she was a twenty-nine-year-old seasoned stage actress with a lot of spunk—but something less than a spectacular career. She had played on Broadway in a leading role (once), married a financial backer whom she later sued for bigamy, written a play that had gone nowhere, and started her own theater company that was to tour the entire Caribbean . . . but ran out of money in Havana.

In 1891 Fuller landed the female lead in a new, slyly titled melodrama, *Quack, M.D.* "While we were at work," she wrote in

79

her autobiography, "the author got the idea of adding to the play a scene in which Dr. Quack hypnotized a young widow. Hypnotism at that moment was very much to the fore in New York."

Having already spent all the money advanced to her for costumes, she scrounged through her wardrobe and found a long silk skirt that an admiring British lieutenant had once sent to her from India. Desperate, she hoped no one would take too much notice of the ridiculous-looking garment in the green light that was to flood the garden scenery, where the widow character she played was to be seduced by evil Dr. Quack.

Doing a little impromptu choreography during the hypnosis scene, Fuller fluttered around the stage, holding her arms up high because "my robe was so long that I was continually stepping on it." The audience more than took notice of Fuller and her diaphanous gown; the scene brought the house down. Playing it for all it was worth, Fuller continued with her ad-libbed antics and prompted twenty encores. The critics panned the play the next day but loved Fuller, although she was quite unsure "how to make the most of it."

The next morning, she put the gown on "to make sure of what I had done the evening before." As she stood before her dressing mirror, the amber morning light illuminated the cloth. "Golden reflections played in the folds of the sparkling silk, and in this light my body was vaguely revealed in shadowy contour. This was a moment of intense emotion. Unconsciously I realized that I was in the presence of a great discovery. I had created a new dance."

Hyperbole aside, she realized that, if handled carefully, the "new dance" could be her meal ticket and a way to fulfill her life-long ambition to perform on the great stages of Europe. Having never trained as a dancer, the amply figured Fuller figured she would have to give Mother Nature all the help she could muster. By necessity, then, she created lighting apparatuses with carefully arranged red, blue, and yellow lights that dramatized her billowing costumes. Her lighting equipment, as well as her wardrobe, traveled everywhere she did.

In this day of laser-assisted special effects, Fuller's invention seems simplistic. But in the late nineteenth century, when she began her show, lighting was merely considered a way to illuminate the stage, or, as in the case of the notorious *Quack, M.D.,* a crude attempt at coloration (green equals garden). Fuller was the first to use color and light as an aesthetic element in theater.

Loie Fuller went on to become lavishly famous. While even the most generous reviewers were discreet enough to overlook her dancing technique, artists and royalty throughout Europe flocked to see her performance of *The Dance of the Butterfly, The Dance of the Serpentine,* and *The Dance of the Flowers.* Sarah Bernhardt copied her lighting designs. Auguste Rodin called her "a genius." Critics hailed her as "a revolutionist in art." Ruth St. Denis was inspired by her use of drapery and light, and to Isadora Duncan, whom Loie later brought to Europe to launch her career, Fuller was undoubtedly a mentor.

She never stopped experimenting with light. She was the first to use phosphorescent material on stage, and for her "Fire Dance" she performed on a pane of glass illuminated from below to create a flamelike effect. In 1927, at age sixty-five, she gave her last public performance, *Shadow Ballet,* which incorporated cinematic lighting effects. She died a few months later, in Paris, of pneumonia.

Mary Elizabeth Hallock Greenewalt, like Loie Fuller, was an artist before she became an inventor. Born in Beirut, Syria, in 1871, she was the daughter of the U.S. consul there. It appears her inventive spirit came not from her parents but from her grandfather, who had invented the first practical type for printing in Arabic.

A gifted student of music, Mary studied at the Philadelphia Musical Academy, where at age twenty-two she won a gold medal for her piano performance in 1893. She went on to tour as a soloist with the Pittsburgh and Philadelphia symphony orchestras for many years, and she gave recitals by herself across the country. Recognized internationally as the leading interpreter of Chopin, she recorded several of the composer's works for Columbia Records between 1919 and 1920.

Around the turn of the century, Greenewalt became interested in color and how it emotionally and physiologically affected the viewer and, carrying it one step farther, the listener. History doesn't record what inspired her, but it may have been the first published works on color associations by early psychologists, or the beginning of the avant-garde movement in orchestrated music. (It was around this same period that Arnold Schoenberg began experimenting with his twelve-tone musical scale.) In any event, she began to relate the beat of the metronome to the human heartbeat and the colors of the spectrum to the seven notes of the diatonic scale. Finally, she theorized that the listening experience could be heightened if the music were accompanied with its mathematical equivalents of light and color.

She was ready to hit the stage and put her theory into action when she realized that technology was not quite ready for her. So in 1905, obtaining U.S. patent No. 1,357,773, she constructed her own rheostat, a mechanism for varying the intensity of light produced by incandescent bulbs. She began delivering lectures on her theory of pulse and rhythm, and she published several articles on the subject.

In 1916 she presented in triumphal manner to the national convention of the Illuminating Society of Engineers the culmination of fifteen years' work—the Sarabet. Describing it as a "light-and-color player," the Sarabet consisted of on-off switches and rheostats configured like a piano keyboard, which allowed the operator to vary the color and light intensity in an auditorium. Subsequent developments in lighting technology soon made the Sarabet obsolete, but her idea of relating music to color and light has become an essential element in performance art and the live shows of avant-garde pop musicians such as Laurie Anderson and Peter Gabriel. Truly ahead of her time, Greenewalt was the first multimedia artist.

Jean Rosenthal, Broadway's most respected lighting designer, wasn't interested in bringing her craft to the attention of the audience. In fact, she was once quoted as saying that "the most successful and brilliant work a lighting designer does is usually the least noticeable."

Despite the great strides that had been made in theatrical

lighting since the turn of the century, even in the early 1930s there was nothing called "lighting design." A lighting technician was expected to install the lights and nothing more.

Rosenthal got her first chance to spread her wings when she was hired by Orson Welles to be in charge of lighting for the Mercury Theatre. Her work began to get special attention in 1937, when critics took notice of the dramatic lighting for Welles's updated *Julius Caesar*. Her halcyon days on Broadway were from the late 1950s to the late 1960s, during which she served as lighting designer for *West Side Story* (1957), *Becket* (1960), *Hello, Dolly!* (1964), *Fiddler on the Roof* (1964), *Hamlet* (with Richard Burton, 1964), *The Odd Couple* (1965), *Cabaret* (1966), and *Plaza Suite* (1968).

Ironically, commercial theater never was her first love, and she always gave first priority to her longtime association with Martha Graham's dance company. Rosenthal also designed lighting for the New York City Ballet and for the opera season at New York City Center. In addition, she designed the lighting for a number of important buildings, including the Pan American terminal at John F. Kennedy International Airport and the entire Los Angeles Music Center.

She is credited for introducing two-dimensional lighting to the stage by illuminating from the side as well as from above and below. She also created a whole new palette of pastel-colored lights for the stage. But her most enduring contribution to lighting design was her invention of a lighting notation system. She realized that lighting design lacked a "specific and orderly attitude." If theatrical lighting were to become an artistic discipline, "there must be a technique and a method for organizing" ideas.

When she began at the Federal Theatre project, there was no way for one lighting "technician" to replicate the work of another, no method of recording which types of lights were used in what arrangement and when during a performance. What began as cue notes to herself was eventually adopted by the profession as its universal language. John Houseman, one of the creative giants of American theater, credited her with no less than "bringing organization and order into the lighting of shows."

Suffering from terminal cancer in 1969, Rosenthal, the quin-

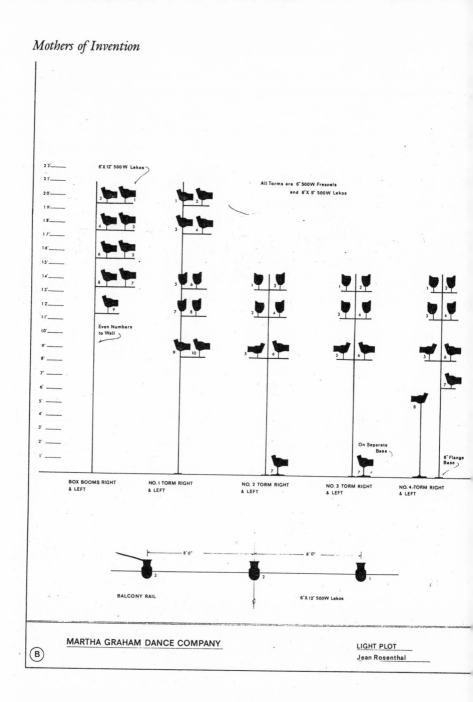

MARTHA GRAHAM DANCE COMPANY

LIGHT PLOT
Jean Rosenthal

With this schematic diagram, any production of Hello Dolly *can precisely duplicate the original Broadway stage lighting. Before Jean Rosenthal developed her annotation system, lighting designers were left in the dark.*

tessential professional, had herself taken by wheelchair into the theater to complete the lighting design for a new Martha Graham dance. Rosenthal once and for all established that theatrical lighting was more than just illumination but also an artistic element that can affect "how you see what you see, how you feel about it, and how you hear what you are hearing."

Just for Fun/Trivial Pursuits

NECESSITY ISN'T THE only mother of invention; pure frippery has led to the creation of life's many small pleasures. Where would we be without Elizabeth Flanagan's cocktail, Ruth Wakefield's chocolate chip cookie, or the hundreds of dolls and toys that have been patented by fun-loving women? And what about the great majority of women inventors, whose products, though fascinating, will never make anyone's Hall of Fame?

Ruth Handler

THE BARBIE DOLL

Barbie and Ken Handler, children of Mattel, Inc., founders Elliot and Ruth Handler, weren't named after two famous dolls. Rather, the dolls were named after the children. Ruth Handler came up with the idea of the glamorous Barbie fashion doll and named it for her young daughter. Later, the boyfriend doll was named for the Handlers' son.

Ruth Handler is an American success story right out of Horatio Alger. Born in Denver, Colorado, and married to her high-school sweetheart in 1938, Handler moved to Los Angeles on an impulse, turning a summer vacation into a job at Paramount Studios. "I was visiting someone at the studio for lunch," Handler recalls, "and on impulse applied for a job. I was told they were virtually impossible to get, but I was hired the same day. I don't take no for an answer."

While Ruth Handler worked as a secretary, Elliot Handler attended art school and designed lighting fixtures, building furniture for their home in his spare time. "My bright young wife stated if I could make these for the house, why not make some for sale?" he recalled in 1967. Soon the Handler furniture business was grossing $2 million a year. And that was only the beginning.

With scraps of wood and metal from the shop, Elliot Handler, at his wife's suggestion, began making dollhouse furniture. Mattel Creations (named for then-partner Harold *Mat*son and *El*-liot Handler) expanded by 1946 into a toy firm making miniature wood and plastic tables and chairs. In 1947 a toy ukulele that Elliot designed—and, later, a toy piano—brought the firm into the mainstream of national toy manufacturers. He soon patented an inexpensive, durable music box mechanism, the first American-made competition to costly Swiss imports. A patented automatic cap gun, again Elliot's contribution, helped the firm to gross $5 million by 1955, when it became the first toy company to use television advertising on the brand-new *Mickey Mouse Club* program.

But it was 1959, and an invention by Ruth Handler, that brought the Mattel company international fame and quadrupled its sales.

"Through years of observing our daughter's play patterns with dolls," remembered Elliot Handler, "my wife noted that she invariably passed by dolls of her own age group, favoring instead teenage dolls with fashion accessories. At the time, the only such teenage dolls were paper cutouts." Ruth's idea was to create a grown-up doll, a model for authentic clothing and accessories, a surrogate for a little girl's fantasies of her future. The reception to Barbie—named after the Handlers' daughter—at the 1959 New York Toy Show was cool. "You're out of your mind; it won't sell" was what Ruth heard.

Barbie sold $500 million worth in her first eight years.

"I guess I learned to observe people in their daily lives," says Ruth Handler, "and, every once in a while, I identify a need." The Barbie name was copyrighted and some mechanical features of the doll were patented, but Ruth Handler's name doesn't appear on a patent that says "Barbie doll." "I didn't actually sculpt Barbie or sew her dresses," says Ruth with a smile, "I set down the specifications and approved everything, but the physical work was done by others. I manage the process of creating the design, and then assign engineers and technicians to make them. The patents end up in their names, assigned to the company. Very seldom is the boss named as the inventor. The boss has to know what the final product is to be. When you know the characteristics you're looking for, you get technicians to make it happen."

Ruth Handler became vice-president of Mattel, Inc., from 1948 to 1967 and later president from 1967 to 1973. She was a founding member of the Los Angeles Music Center, a member of the National Business Council for Consumer Affairs, a director of the Federal Reserve Bank of San Francisco, a member of the Presidential Advisory Committee on the Economic Role of Women, and a guest professor at UCLA and USC. But it wasn't always easy to be accepted as a woman in these prestigious roles.

"I remember one time," says Handler, "when a brokerage company was holding a meeting with the investment community at a private club. My husband and I arrived, and two men from the brokerage grabbed each of us, leading my husband off in one direction and me in another. I was taken through the kitchen, through the garbage area, and down a back hall. Eventually I ended up in the meeting room, where my husband had already been seated for some five minutes. Then I realized: I was being snuck into this room, violating club rules which don't allow women. And I was lead speaker, president of the company, and the guest of honor!"

By the early 1970s, the idea of a woman company president was a little easier to accept. Ruth Handler was, by then, cochairman of the board. But she also suffered a life-shattering tragedy, a tragedy that came at a time when Mattel, Inc., was suffering financial reversals. Ruth Handler was diagnosed as having breast cancer, and she underwent radical mastectomy of the left breast. Unnerved, disfigured—"unwomanized," as she put it—Ruth retired from Mattel.

But the woman who made her fortune by targeting the needs of the consumer had lifetime habits that brought her out of her sadness. Unable to find a breast prosthesis that was natural and comfortable, she worked with prosthetic designer Peyton Massey and some retired Mattel technicians to develop the Nearly Me line of breast prostheses for mastectomies. Ruthton, Inc., owned and operated by Ruth Handler, now manufactures and distributes her designs of breast replacements and specially designed swimwear to cancer victims around the country. And Ruth Handler found a second career—a second career as an inventor, yet—that brought her a satisfaction she never expected.

"The first half of my life, Mattel, was very rewarding, very exciting," says Handler. "It grew very fast, and because of that I had to remain in a somewhat impersonal role as related to my consumer. We sat in an ivory tower, viewed children through one-way mirrors, and acted on information supplied by market researchers.

"This time, I'm doing the whole thing my way. I make my own decisions, I make my own mistakes. But most of all, I stand there toe-to-toe with my consumer. I fit the product on her body. These women come to me hostile, angry, confused, and full of tears, suffering a terrible blow to their self-esteem. To see that frown turn to a smile . . . it's very gratifying. I never got that close to people before. Now, on a daily basis, I feel very close to everyone."

Barbara "Barbie" Handler Segal and Kenneth "Ken" Handler have given Ruth and Elliot Handler five grandchildren—but this grandmother sees no retirement in sight. At age sixty-nine, Handler is still running the Ruthton Corporation and maintaining a nationwide business itinerary.

Ruth Wakefield

CHOCOLATE CHIP COOKIE

Restaurateur Ruth Wakefield created the chocolate chip cookie in a time-honored fashion: by accident. It was 1933, and the owner of the Toll House Inn at Whitman, Massachusetts, was preparing a batch of chocolate butter drops. Hoping to save a little preparation time, Ruth decided to forgo melting chocolate squares for the batter, but rather break a semisweet candy bar into pieces and throw it in the mix. The chocolate chunks, she assumed, would

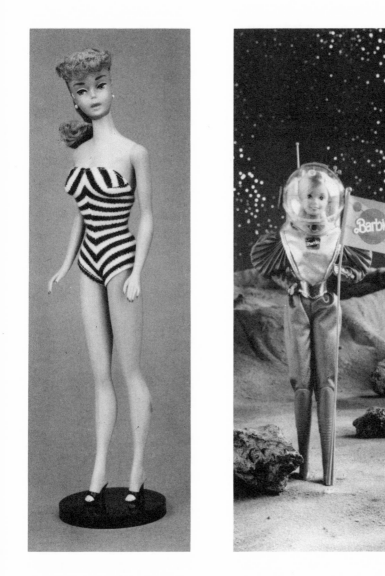

Barbie has gone through many changes since Ruth Handler thought her up in 1959. But she's still a living doll. Barbie doll with original pronged stand, © Mattel 1959. Astronaut™ Barbie® doll, © Mattel, Inc. 1986.

melt in the heat of the oven. To her surprise, the chocolate morsels stayed firm in the finished cookie—and the final "mistake" was delicious. She named her invention the Toll House cookie, and it became the business's calling card.

The Toll House Inn is a piece of Cape Cod history: Built in 1709, it began as a rest stop for horses on the Bedford–Boston route. Ruth Graves Wakefield and her husband, Kenneth, bought the building in 1930 and opened a restaurant. Ruth had previously worked as a dietician and food lecturer, and her menus always stressed natural and wholesome foods presented with variety and balance. The Toll House prospered; rated four stars in regional guidebooks, it provided a comfortable living for the Wakefields.

As the Toll House chocolate chip cookie grew in popularity, the Nestlé candy company began scoring its chocolate bars, for easier breaking. In 1939 Nestlé began distributing chocolate "morsels," specifically for inclusion in Ruth's recipe. The company also bought the rights to the Toll House name (although a recipe always is in the public domain) and registered it as a trademark. According to a Nestlé company representative, "In addition to various payments, Mrs. Wakefield was also supplied with chocolate."

The Wakefields sold Toll House Inn in 1966 to a family who tried, unsuccessfully, to turn it into a trendy night spot. In 1970 the then-abandoned inn was bought by the Saccone family, who restored it to its original ambience. Even though the centuries-old structure burned to the ground on New Year's Eve 1984, the Saccones continue to make original recipe Toll House cookies in a bakery a few miles down the road. Currently the Toll House annex produces thirty-three thousand cookies a day, and it expects to increase that number considerably after the historical tavern is rebuilt.

The entire chocolate morsel industry is a result of Ruth Wakefield's misfired shortcut. Today, ninety million bags of chocolate morsels are sold each year, representing 150 million pounds of cookies—enough cookies annually to circle the globe ten times.

Here is the 1936 version of the classic recipe:

Ruth Wakefield's Chocolate Crunch Cookies

Cream
1 cup butter, add
¾ cup brown sugar
¾ cup granulated sugar and
2 eggs beaten. Dissolve
1 tsp. baking soda in
1 tsp. hot water, and mix in
2¼ cups flour sifted with
1 tsp. salt. Lastly add

1 cup chopped nuts and
2 bars (7-oz.) Nestlé's yellow label chocolate, semisweet, cut into pieces the size of a pea Flavor with
1 tsp. vanilla and drop in half teaspoons on a greased cookie sheet. Bake 10 to 12 minutes at 375°. Makes 100 cookies.

Anonymous

ICE CREAM CONE

The event is documented, but the name of the young woman who invented the ice cream cone has somehow been misplaced. It was in 1904, at the Louisiana Purchase Exposition at St. Louis, Missouri, that an ice cream salesman named Charles Menches was courting a certain unnamed lady. One day, the ardent gentleman brought his date both a bouquet of flowers and an ice cream sandwich, and she couldn't find a way to hold both of them at the same time. She took the biscuit from the top of the ice cream sandwich, and wrapped it around the flowers as a makeshift vase. She took the other half of the cookie wafer and wrapped it around the ice cream, to keep it from dripping on her dress. Thus was the ice cream cone born.

It was a matter of days before a souvenir salesman at the ex-

93

position, Abe Doumar of New Jersey, mentioned the idea to an ice cream vendor in the midway, suggesting that the vendor could charge more money for the product and save money on ice cream dishes at the same time. The Doumar family still dispenses ice cream cones at Coney Island, and Charles Menches's companion is still anonymous.

Elizabeth Flanagan

THE COCKTAIL

Elizabeth "Betsy" Flanagan is as much a part of folk legend as history, but the tale of the origin of the cocktail has been preserved with so few variations that there seems little doubt as to its authenticity.

Betsy Flanagan was a tavernkeeper somewhere in New England during the American Revolutionary War. Her inn was frequented by rebel officers and soldiers, many of whom sat around complaining about a local Tory fat cat who prospered while they suffered.

One night, Betsy created a special drink for her "regulars": She mixed rum and fruit juice, and she decorated each glass with a feather plucked from their enemy's rooster. The crowd loved both the jest and the mixed drink, which got its name when a young French officer shouted out, "*Vive le coq*'s tail!"

Nicole-Barbe Clicquot

CHAMPAGNE STORAGE

In the early nineteenth century, Mme. Nicole-Barbe Clicquot revolutionized winemaking by devising a method of clarifying sparkling wine and champagne. The young Frenchwoman, widowed at age twenty, invented a process that is still in use today; she also invented the first pink champagne.

Champagne bottled before 1800 would hardly be recognizable to a present-day connoisseur. Dom Perignon, cellarmaster of the Benedictine abbey of Hautvillers from 1668 to 1715, is credited with making the first sparkling wine that we now know as champagne. But even the gifted French monk could not devise a way of removing the natural sediment that settled to the bottom of the bottles without losing the effervescence. So for a hundred years—until Madame Clicquot instituted *sur pointe* storage—champagne was cloudy and gritty.

Born in 1777 to upper-class parents, Nicole grew up in the ancient city of Reims, which borders the gentle rolling hills of the Champagne district. The idyllic surroundings of her childhood contrasted sharply with the turbulent political climate in France between the Revolution and the rise of Napoleon.

In 1794 she was betrothed to one M. Clicquot, who, twenty years earlier, had opened a moderately successful champagne winery and shipping firm. Within two years, right after the birth of their daughter, M. Clicquot died. To the surprise of the Champagne establishment, Nicole—or La Veuve ("The Widow") Clicquot, as

95

she would thereafter be known—vowed to continue the business herself. Most predicted she would be penniless in two years.

Beyond her youth and gender, Mme. Clicquot faced other hardships. The champagne industry itself was crumbling. Connoisseurs considered it a fad: How could one take seriously a wine that had the clarity of yesterday's dishwater? And Napoleon's growing appetite for the European landscape had reduced exports to a trickle, created massive business taxes, and thrown the French currency into a tailspin.

She couldn't do anything about the Napoleonic wars (although the fact that her father, M. Ponsardin, was the mayor of Reims and a close ally of Napoleon did help to lighten the Clicquot tax load). To help in marketing, La Veuve took on a partner, a naturalized Frenchman from Germany. M. Werle would eventually become president of the local chamber of commerce and, still later, succeed Nicole's father as mayor of Reims.

Nicole focused her energy on the immediate problem at hand: improving the quality of champagne. Champagne is bubbly because, during the fermentation process, yeast and sugar are added to the bottles. This creates fizz but leaves sediment behind. Every time vintners tried to drain the sediment, the effervescence would escape, too.

Under the *remuage* ("moving") method that Clicquot invented, the corked champagne bottles are stored upside down, or *sur pointe*. Over the course of several months, individual bottles are shaken and turned daily, and the sediment gradually slides down to rest against the cork. At the right moment, the bottle is opened for an instant: the pressure expels the sediment, and the cork is quickly reinserted.

Making pink champagne turned out to be much easier: La Veuve simply pressed the grapes as soon as they were picked.

So successful were these innovations that Clicquot's sales figures soared ahead of her competitors'. She and her partner were largely responsible for creating a demand for champagne in the European capitals, and for breaking the import duties imposed by England.

Rich by her own invention, Mme. Clicquot retired in 1820 at

age forty-three to the grand Château de Boursault, where she lived graciously for nearly half a century more. Her daughter grew up to marry the Comte de Cevigne. Today the Clicquot vineyard, third largest champagne house in France, is run by descendants of the Werle family, but labels still bear the name of La Veuve Clicquot-Ponsardin. You can order a bottle in fine restaurants around the world.

Rose O'Neill

THE KEWPIE DOLL

From 1912 to 1914, the Kewpie doll was an absolute craze. People were buying Kewpie books and Kewpie rattles, Kewpie soap and Kewpie dishes, Kewpie pianos and Kewpie salt-and-pepper shakers. Women began plucking their eyebrows to mimic the surprised dot brows of the little porcelain cherubs. Poet/artist Rose Cecil O'Neill made $1.5 million from the munchkin dolls, which she first invented as magazine illustrations and patented in 1913.

Rose O'Neill was born in 1874 in Wilkes-Barre, Pennsylvania. Throughout her childhood, she was encouraged in her artistic bent, and at age fourteen won a drawing contest sponsored by the *World Herald* newspaper in Omaha (where the family then lived). Soon she began seeing her cartoons and illustrations published in midwestern newspapers and magazines.

Seeking a wider audience for her art, O'Neill moved to New York City in 1893. She referred to city dwellers as "the wolves," however, and looked forward to her stays at the family's retirement estate in the Ozarks, called Bonnie Brook. There she married

Gray Latham in 1896 and began signing her drawings "Latham O'Neill." Many readers assumed Latham O'Neill was a man.

By this time, Rose was selling her drawings to *Puck* and *Life* magazines. After her divorce from Latham in 1901, she began an intense correspondence with her editor at *Puck,* Harry Leon Wilson, and married him in 1902.

The Wilsons lived in an opulent literary whirl. Rose wrote a novel called *The Loves of Edwy* (Harper, 1904), and Harry wrote a best seller, *The Spenders.* Harry also collaborated with Booth Tarkington on *The Man from Home,* which was a hit Broadway play, and it was thanks to Tarkington (albeit indirectly) that the Kewpie doll was created.

Tarkington had presented the Wilsons with a white bulldog, which became a spoiled house pet. As her first attempt at pottery, Rose made a bisque statuette of the pup, calling the piece "Kewpie Doodle Dog." After separating from Harry Wilson in 1907, Rose began using the cute Kewpie concept in her stories and drawings for *The Ladies' Home Journal.*

The little Kewpies from Kewpieville did good deeds like keeping birds' eggs warm and recovering lost babies; they were immediate sentimental favorites of the magazine's readership. *Ladies' Home Journal* publisher Edward Bok suggested that Rose begin making bisque dolls of the Kewpies, which were first manufactured in Germany. Rose gained fame for visiting overseas factory workers and telling them to be extra careful with the tiniest dolls "because they were for the poorest children."

Porcelain and bisque Kewpie dolls began being manufactured in Belgium and France after the outbreak of war; celluloid, wood, and paper models were made in the United States. With her royalties, Rose bought a home in New York's bohemian Greenwich Village and a villa on the island of Capri. She upgraded the Bonnie Brook estate in the Ozarks, calling it "a good place to unbutton." Rose considered herself a patroness of the arts, holding salons for poets and sculptors. She liked to appear in public wearing flowing robes and in bare feet, and she launched a second career writing romantic poetry and Gothic novels.

Rose O'Neill went through her entire fortune by 1936, and

she returned to the Ozarks to spend her last years at Bonnie Brook with her devoted sister, Callista. Rose completed her memoirs in 1944, and she died that same year of heart failure at age seventy.

TRIVIAL PURSUITS

Somewhere between the creators of the brassiere and the electron diffractor lie the many women whose inventions were destined for anonymity from the start. The U.S. Patent Office is filled with devices made obsolete by a superior gadget almost before the ink was dry on the application. Others were too specialized to the creator's personal needs, lacking that necessary quality of universality that marked the paper bag or the Toidy Seat.

Some inventions are relegated to obscurity because they're so difficult to market. Frances Gabe's "self-cleaning house" is difficult to retail. Dr. Elizabeth French's patented "appliances for treating the human body electrically," which she exhibited at the World's Columbian Exposition in Chicago in 1893, would never get approved today by the FDA, nor would Dr. Katherine Perlman's synthetic cannabis. And Mrs. Gladys Ritter's expandable jock strap (Patent No. 4,526,167), with its "elongated soft cloth envelope for an erect male organ," is every advertising agency's nightmare.

Last, there were those inventors who thought to improve upon Nature's own design and who took an Icarian nose dive into ignominy. The best intentions of Sarah Ruth, Deniece Lemiere, and Bertha Dlugi notwithstanding, if God had wanted horses to have sun shades, dogs to have spectacles, and parakeets to have diapers, she would have designed them herself.

Yet all these women and thousands more unmentioned deserve praise for exercising an ingenuity basic to all of us. Someone once wrote that "the distinguishing characteristic of the human species is that we invent." These are some very human ladies.

Mary Peck Butterworth

DISPOSABLE COUNTERFEITING
PLATES

Mary Butterworth could hardly patent her 1716 invention; it was, after all, highly illegal. But it certainly was an effective device, and it did its job perfectly. Not only did Mrs. Butterworth make a comfortable living from counterfeiting, but also she was never convicted of the crime because her disposable printing plates left no evidence behind.

Daughter of a Colonial innkeeper who lived in Rehoboth, Massachusetts, Butterworth began counterfeiting Rhode Island currency in a kitchen workshop. (In those days, colonies produced different monies, but the notes of one colony were still spendable in another.) Butterworth had contrived a method of counterfeiting £5 notes using a sheet of muslin cloth instead of a copper plate. According to the testimony of an alleged accomplice, the master counterfeiter placed a piece of "fine watter starched musoline" on a genuine bill, "and so pucked out the letters upon said musoline," which was then pressed with a hot iron onto a piece of currency-style paper. The image was transferred to the plain paper, enhanced with quill pen-and-ink, and the incriminating muslin "plates" were burned immediately.

Butterworth's funny money was passed around Rehoboth by a ring that included Butterworth relatives and even the Rehoboth town clerk. The ring prospered throughout Plymouth Colony for almost a decade. The bogus currency sold for half its face value, and it circulated with little suspicion until 1722.

In that year, neighboring townships became interested in the Peck/Butterworth fortune (Butterworth's husband had recently built a grandiose home for his family) and sent a sheriff to sniff around. No counterfeiting plates were discovered, and it was only because of an accomplice's confession that charges were leveled at all. Mary Peck Butterworth and her brother, Israel Peck, were brought before a grand jury at Bristol, Massachusetts, in September 1723, but charges were dropped due to the lack of tangible evidence.

Mary Peck Butterworth lived to eighty-nine years of age, bore seven children, and died in her bed at Rehoboth, a respected matron of the community but with a saucy past.

Frances Gabe

SELF-CLEANING HOUSE

It's hard to tell which Frances Gabe of Newton, Oregon, hates more: the housecleaning or the dirt. Either way, she has effectively quashed both foes with the Gabe self-cleaning house.

More like a car wash than a traditional dwelling, the Gabe house would come equipped with a general Cleaning, Drying, Heating, and Cooling apparatus in each room. "Approximately ten inches square, it fits snugly to the ceiling," says Frances. "Resembling a handsome light fixture, the unit lends itself to any decorative motif." When a room gets dirty, just turn on the CDHC, and gallons of soapy water pour forth, followed by a clean-water rinse and a forced, hot-air drying. "It also has the capability of dispensing roomwide germicide or insect spray," she notes.

What about the books, the bedclothes, the baubles? No problem; Gabe's got them covered. "In the bedrooms, there is a long narrow bolster at the head of the bed that opens to shield the bedding from the cleaning soap and water." *Objects d'art* are stored in nonmetallic canisters with waterguard lids. "Books, too, have been provided for," says Frances, although she is vague about the provisions.

For those hard-to-get spots, there is a small, mobile apparatus called the auxiliary spot cleaner concealed in every room, which also dispenses soapy or clear rinse water.

Frances also has designed time-saving appurtenances for the Gabe house: a combination water heater/bathtub-warmer, a self-cleaning toilet, bookshelves that dust themselves, and a dish-washer/kitchen cupboard that never has to be unloaded. The most ingenious is the multipurpose Gabe clothes freshener, self-cleaning closet, and shower bath. "The soiled wash-and-wear clothing is hung in the clothes freshener and the control dial is set. That's it! When the clothing is ready to be worn again, it is fresh and where it belongs," she says.

Ideally situated between the bedroom and the bathroom, the device also serves as a "luxury shower bath." "It's not necessary to soap oneself. The same cleaning cycle used for washing and rinsing the clothing is used for the bath," she says. To really save time, people could conceivably shower and launder their clothes simultaneously.

If the Gabe house begins to sound like Rube Goldberg's worst nightmare, at least one professional association of inventors—Inventors Workshop International—has lavished praise on it: "Once every few years," they wrote in their magazine *The Lightbulb,* "an individual inventor comes along whose innovativeness is so advanced, prolific, and inspiring that we are compelled to give every aid, encouragement, and support it is within our power to do."

Frances began work on her self-cleaning house in 1955 and is still perfecting it. She has filed sixty-eight patents for the project and invested more than $15,000 of her own money. It's obviously not for everyone—you have to be a big fan of polyester suits, for one thing—yet Gabe is convinced that the invention has commercial value. "Women throughout the country," she says, "who have heard of the self-cleaning house are impatient to see this dream become a reality."

Penny Cooper

FLAT FOOD POUCH

Samuel Coleridge dreamed about the "pleasure dome of Kubla Khan"; Penny Cooper dreamed about a plastic pouch of dried beef stew. "The stew I dreamed about tasted so delicious when I poured it into a pot and added hot water that I knew my idea was something that could be made to work," she said.

Cooper hopes to do for the food industry what "scratch and sniff" pictures did for the perfume trade. Wouldn't you love to taste-test that new pound cake/chili/imported caviar? Wouldn't the manufacturer love for you to do so?

In January 1985, Penny Cooper received Patent No. 4,492,305 for what the U.S. Patent Office calls "magazine page dehydrated foods in plastic bags." Penny prefers "flat food pouch." It's the first invention of the forty-three-year-old New Yorker, who works as an administrative assistant for a nonprofit organization.

She describes her invention as "an advertising/promotional/ marketing device," a removable pouch "containing dehydrated food and faced with an advertisement bound into the spine of a magazine to form a page within the same." The pouch would be closed with pressure-sensitive seams (like a Ziploc bag) and is removable via a Velcro-like binding.

"Of course, it's fun to fantasize what I'd do if I could sell my

United States Patent [19]

Cooper et al.

[11] **Patent Number:** **4,492,306**

[45] **Date of Patent:** **Jan. 8, 1985**

[54] **MAGAZINE PAGE DEHYDRATED FOODS IN PLASTIC BAGS**

[75] Inventors: **Penny S. Cooper,** 336 W. 71st St., New York, N.Y. 10023; **Richard L. Miller,** Dix Hills, N.Y.

[73] Assignee: **Penny S. Cooper,** New York, N.Y.

[21] Appl. No.: **571,334**

[22] Filed: **Jan. 16, 1984**

[51] **Int. Cl.³** **B65D 27/00; B65D 85/72**
[52] **U.S. Cl.** **206/216;** 206/232; 206/472; 206/525
[58] **Field of Search** 206/216, 232, 472, 484, 206/525; 383/38, 100

[56] **References Cited**

U.S. PATENT DOCUMENTS

1,689,637	10/1928	Mordecai	206/232
2,801,002	7/1957	Volckening et al.	206/472
4,369,882	1/1983	Schlugee	206/216
4,433,783	2/1984	Dickinson	383/38

Primary Examiner—William T. Dixson, Jr.
Attorney, Agent, or Firm—Richard L. Miller

[57] **ABSTRACT**

An advertising/promotional/marketing/device. A removed pouch containing dehydrated food and faced with advertisement bound into the spline of a magazine to form a page within same. The pouch is assembled by use of pressure sensitive seams and ZIPLOC ® closures. The page is removable from the magazine by simple tearing or releasing of VELCRO ® binding.

5 Claims, 3 Drawing Figures

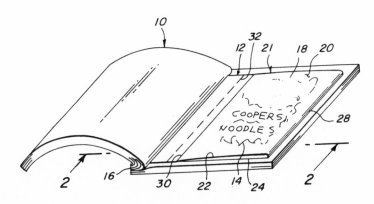

The actual patent application filed by Penny Cooper for the flat food pouch. She thoug it would be an improvement over scratch-and-sniff magazine advertisements. But t U.S. Postal Service disagreed.

invention for a lot of money," says Penny. "But I have no idea what to expect. I don't even know what kind of fees I'd charge anyone who was interested."

Madison Avenue cynics predict an early demise for the Cooper food pouch. In a recent *New York Times* article, one magazine consultant bluntly opined, "It might be of interest, but production-wise it would be horrendous in cost, especially for any kind of mass media." Another called it "too prohibitive in terms of cost." A third said the post office would object to manufacturers' food samples being mailed at magazine postal rates. And then there's the potential problem of tampering.

Even if the flat food pouch remains a pipe dream, Penny has other inventive possibilities. Recently she dreamed about a diagonal elevator. . . .

Amanda Theodosia Jones

VACUUM CANNING

Amanda Theodosia Jones was a prolific inventor but not a very successful one. Nine patents in the field of vacuum canning led to formation of her U.S. Women's Pure Food Vacuum Preserving Company in Chicago, a feminist experiment whose control was wrested from her in only three years. Her inventions in oil heating—which she said came to her through psychic contact—were never commercially viable. Although her vacuum canning methods were used widely for half a century, she never received any particular credit for them and was known best as a poet and spiritualist.

Nonetheless, Jones at one point operated canning plants in

both Illinois and Wisconsin, and her "Jones exhauster" (Patent Nos. 139,547; 139,580; and 140,247) canning machine was a breakthrough in food preservation. She was the first safely to preserve fresh food in quantity without first cooking all the flavor out of it.

Amanda Jones was born in 1835 to a family of twelve children in upstate New York. Her father was a weaver who considered books "more necessary than daily bread." By age fifteen Amanda was teaching at Buffalo High School, in the city where her family moved in 1845.

Amanda was a sickly child, and a bout of tuberculosis in 1859 left her a semi-invalid forever seeking rest cures. By this time, however, she was already a recognized poet, writing for the *Methodist Ladies' Repository* of Cincinnati. In 1861 her book *Utah, and Other Poems* was published, followed in 1867 by *Poems*.

After a long relapse of her tuberculosis and the sudden death of her brother, Amanda turned to spiritualism, considering herself a bona fide medium and traveling around the country giving séances in the homes of well-to-do believers. She continued to write during this period and worked for magazines including *Western Rural, Universe,* and *Interior.*

In 1872 Miss Jones conceived of a vacuum process for preserving food, in which fresh food was placed in a container, the air was drained out through a series of valves, and hot (100–120° F) liquid was added to the jar, which was immediately sealed. She had five patents issued in that year and the one following—three of them copatented with a cousin, L. C. Cooley (some histories refer to him as an "in-law").

The U.S. Women's Pure Food Vacuum Preserving Company was founded in 1890 and utilized Jones's methods to produce rice and tapioca puddings, as well as a line of lunch meats. All the officers, stockholders, and employees (except the fellow who stoked the boiler and Amanda's copatentee relative) were female. By 1893 Amanda was forced out of management in the firm, and later she sold her interest to a meat-packing concern. (The company, however, thrived until 1923).

Once out of the canning business, Jones returned to the literary life. *A Prairie Idyl* was published in 1882, with four more volumes appearing between 1889 and 1910.

Career changes and relocations were frequent in Jones's life; she said the spirit world often commanded her to pull up stakes. In 1880 she moved to the oil fields of northern Pennsylvania, and there she patented a liquid fuel burner. A proposed business manufacturing these oil burners was unsuccessful, although her research was published in *Engineer* and *Steam Engineering* magazines, and she would go on to receive three more patents in the field.

Amanda Jones did not consider herself a "strident" feminist, although she did affect mannishly short hair and spoke out in favor of women's right to vote. She never married, but lived for many years with the family of one of her sisters. She died in 1914 of influenza at her home in Brooklyn, New York, having remained active—if ill-remunerated—in business well into her seventies. When she was seventy-eight years old, she saw herself listed in *Who's Who in America*.

Mary Nolan

NOLANUM

This was not to be the forty-third improvement in the skirt gauge. Nor would it be still another three-in-one kitchen utensil or a bootjack that doubled as an andiron. And the world by the 1870s had had its fill of foldable beds, desks, rocking chairs, tables, and bathtubs, then the mainstays of distaff inventiveness. No, Mary Nolan's invention would be something much more substantial, infinitely versatile, beautiful in its simplicity, the essence of basicity.

In 1876 Mary Nolan was awarded Patent No. 188,660 for her version of—the brick. She filed the application on December 7, no doubt hoping to capitalize on the Christmas trade (the perfect gift for that someone who has everything?).

Actually, it wasn't a bad invention, and as bricks go it was downright clever. "The object of my invention is to so construct building blocks, that in laying them to form a wall, the blocks of each course shall be laterally locked together, and to the blocks of the other course," she wrote in her patent application. "The blocks are so intimately connected together that the wall will present a uniform surface of finished appearance, so as to render the use of plaster unnecessary for the inner wall of buildings, and otherwise ornamented on the edges for decorative efforts."

She goes on to explain how the bricks—or "improved building blocks," as she calls them—can be made hollow inside for insulation and ventilating purposes. The bricks were also extremely fireproof and durable: "As an instance of this I may state that small hollow bricks of my improved composition have been heated to redness and then suddenly plunged into cold water without affecting them adversely."

And if all this weren't enough, Nolanum could be tinted by "employing glass of different colors in their composition, so that blocks and tiles of the most varied and beautiful character may be produced at but comparatively slight expense."

Even today, this item should leap off Builders' Emporium shelves into the hands of do-it-yourselfers. So why didn't the Nolan brick fly?

That same question, in the context of their own inventions, must have weighed heavily on the minds of all the thousands of women whose applications collect dust in the U.S. Patent Office. In the case of the Nolan brick, one can only speculate. Perhaps it was the fault of a jaded public, wary by this time of anything labeling itself "improved." Maybe it was a concerted campaign by the lumber lords, who saw in Nolanum their own demise. Most likely, the product, like many others, was too expensive to mass-produce, or simply didn't have sufficient structural strength to hold up a roof. But just in case you have seventy-five pounds of kaolin clay lying around, we've reprinted the *patented* formula for Mary Nolan's "improvement in artificial-stone composition." Consider it as an alternative to next year's Christmas fruitcake:

"I take about twenty-five pounds of finely pulverized glass and mix it with about seventy-five pounds of kaolin clay, the mixture being either effected after the kaolin has been reduced to a semifluid condition by admixture with water, or the ingredients may be mixed while in a dry, or nearly dry, condition. After the two ingredients have been stirred together until they become thoroughly and intimately mixed, the composition is then molded into the desired shapes, and the blocks or other objects subsequently baked in a suitable furnace or kiln."

THINGAMAJIGS AND DOOHICKIES

Julia C. Smith received Patent No. 265,164 in 1882 for her compound culinary tool, a combination cake beater, dish cleaner, and plateholder.

Helen G. Gonet of Lynn, Massachusetts, invented an electronic Bible (Patent No. 4,445,196) in 1984 to circumvent "the relatively slow and tedious retrieval of the selected passages, due to the thinness of the pages and small print associated with Bibles generally in use."

May Evans invented a "moustache-guard for attachment to spoons or cups when used in the act of eating soup and other liquid food or drinking coffee" in 1899.

Anna M. Fillspki of Chicago, Illinois, is the coinventor of an antitheft device designed to spring out and draw attention to a thief, causing him or her to drop the stolen item. On May 13, 1975, she received Patent No. 3,882,915.

On July 1, 1975, Bonny B. Koo of Pacific Grove, California, received Patent No. 3,892,412 for a putting practice green "wherein undulations of the surface of the green can be quickly and selectively adjusted and changed at will by the player."

On the same day, Marjoriejean Smith of Walnut, California, was granted Patent No. 3,892,423 for her improved automobile trailer.

Both Bloomingdale's and Bergdorf Goodman have used the patented inflatable mannequin for pantyhose invented by Judith Ann Shackelford and Nancy Rey Cherry.

Mrs. Robert Shields's gauge for cutting lozenges was employed by several large candy companies in the late 1800s.

Elizabeth Stiles invented and marketed a combination desk that could accommodate several users during the day, then be collapsed to a small size for evening meetings. It was displayed at the World Columbian Exposition in 1893.

Sarah H. Bancroft and Sarah W. Tucker built an improved bathing chair for "those who need to bathe their persons and who are too weak to stoop over a basin without a support." They were granted Patent No. 150,510 on May 5, 1874.

In 1969 Pansy Ellen Essman, then forty-eight, patented the Pansy-ette bath aid, a sponge pillow to keep babies secure while they're being washed. Borrowing $30,000, she had the Pansy-ette manufactured and to date has made more than $2 million. "Don't think you're too old to do things. You're never too old," is her advice to budding inventors.

Dorothy Young Kirby of Clermont, Florida, earned $50,000 from her Dot Young sewing guide, which gives homemade clothes a more professional look.

Lillian Huffaker invented a horological device called the ticonometer, which can be used "in many ways to measure business schedules, programs, travel routes, anything measurable by time in hours, minutes, seconds, or fractions." In the 1930s she was the president, director, and chief engineer of Time Controlled

Indicators, Inc., which manufactured her invention.

Dicksie Spolar of Fontana, California, grew tired of trying to guess the amount of spaghetti to cook—she either made too much or too little. So she invented the spaghetti cinch, a tape measure-like device for determining cup servings of cooked spahgetti.

S. Brooks of Helena, Arkansas, was granted Patent No. 187, 695 on February 6, 1877, for her "improvement in the methods of producing lubricated molds in plaster," which enabled the user to model ornamental designs out of butter.

Maria E. Beasley and the Rehfuss brothers of Philadelphia improved the way barrels are made and received a joint patent for their machine on April 10, 1888.

"The object of this invention is to economize or utilize to best advantage the space of closets or wardrobes," wrote Emmeline W. Philbrook about the clothes hook she patented on February 2, 1886 (No. 335,237).

Florella L. Kinsman of Magog, Quebec, filed a U.S. patent in 1881 for a "car-heater"—as in railway car.

Susan Bidwell, along with two coinventors, received Patent No. 163,043 on May 11, 1875, for "an improvement in tooth-brushes."

More than a century later, patents continue to be granted using that very phrase. Just because it's already been done, that doesn't stop you from doing it better. This nation was founded on life, liberty, and the pursuit of a better mousetrap.

SARAH RUTH.

Sun-Shades for Horses.

No. 134,564.   Patented Jan. 7, 1873.

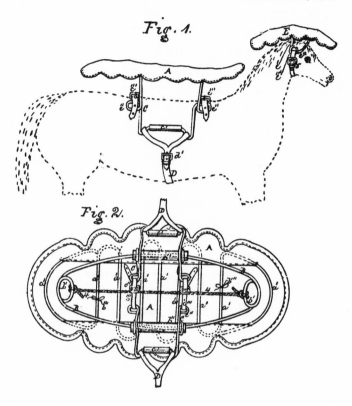

*Sarah Ruth's pony never made the Best Dressed List, as her patent for equine bonnet
was greeted by horse laughs.*

THE SCIENTISTS

The Healers

SOME OF THE first women scientists were physicians. Female folk doctors have been around as long as cuts and bruises, but as early as 1500 B.C. women were studying medicine as a science at the medical school in Heliopolis, Egypt. Two learned women of medicine in ancient Greece—Lais and Sotira—wrote books on abortion and sterility.

Despite intense persecution during the Middle Ages, women refused to abandon either the practice or the scientific study of medicine. The intellectually enlightened city-states of pre-Renaissance Italy had a long tradition of female medical scholars. In the 1300s, Constanza Calenda lectured on medicine at the University of Naples; Dorotea Bocchi succeeded her father as the professor of medicine at the University of Bologna a century later. Convents sometimes provided safe haven for women of medicine: Abbess

Hildegard of Bingen, Germany (1098–1178), encouraged medical research at the convent she founded, and she herself wrote about topics ranging from anatomy to blood circulation.

While by the eighteenth century women were no longer being burned at the stake, they were being barred from medical research institutions. In the early nineteenth century, American women led the Popular Health Movement, which sought to promote midwifery, acquaint the general public with basic home health care, and put an end to such barbaric treatments as bloodletting and calomel (a mercury-based poison) lotion. The movement accomplished many of its goals but could not break the stranglehold of the male medical establishment.

The great lengths women took to practice medicine in the 1800s are illustrated by the extraordinary case of Miranda Stuart, alias Dr. James Barry. She matriculated from Edinburgh College of Medicine in 1812 at age fifteen—as "a frail-looking man"—and entered military service, posing as a male throughout a career that included an appointment as surgeon general of Canada. When an autopsy revealed the late Dr. Barry as the late Miss Stuart, her previously arranged military funeral was canceled. Known for her strict standards on hygiene and diet of the sick, she also discovered, during her service in South Africa, a plant that was widely used to treat syphilis and gonorrhea before the advent of sulfa drugs half a century later.

Elizabeth Blackwell became the first woman ever to receive a medical degree, graduating in 1849 from Geneva Medical College (now Hobart and William Smith Colleges) in Geneva, New York. When her application was placed before the student body, her male peers voted her in as a joke. In 1868 she began the first medical college for women; it remained open until Cornell University began accepting women medical students in 1899. The first major American medical institution to accept women was Johns Hopkins University, which did so in 1897—after accepting an enormous contribution from an heiress on the condition that it begin enrolling women. The first beneficiary of the new policy was Florence Sabin, who conducted pioneering research into blood processes, including the discovery of the origin of red corpuscles.

In the early twentieth century, women scientists were a small but significant force in medical research and disease control. Alice Hamilton, an 1893 graduate of the University of Michigan Medical School, founded the discipline of industrial medicine and saved thousands of workers' lives through her identification of the source of toxic substances in factories and mines. And Edith Quimby developed the field of radiation therapy.

In addition to those featured in this chapter, many other women contributed significant innovations in the field of medicine. Dorothy Mendenhall, who attended Johns Hopkins with Florence Sabin, identified the cell that causes Hodgkin's disease. A French doctor named Suzanne Noel was among the first cosmetic surgeons in the 1920s, and the first to record her procedures.

Cora Downs was the first to identify and establish the cause of tularemia, an infectious disease transmitted by animals. She also was part of a team that perfected the important diagnostic tool of fluorescent antibody staining. Geraldine Thiele invented the first injectable drug to cure shin splints, saving valuable racehorses from an early grave. Her equine preparations also led her to patent a mouthwash that prevents human tooth decay, and she discovered a horse feed that keeps manure from smelling bad.

Lady Mary Bruce worked with her husband in culturing the organism of Malta fever in the 1920s, and she became the first honorary female fellow of the Royal Microscopical Society for her contributions in this often fatal disease. In 1947 Dr. Gerty Cori became the first woman to receive the Nobel Prize in physiology and medicine, which she shared with her husband for their research in carbohydrate metabolism.

Dr. Dorothy Horstman's identification of the polio virus in its early stages was an important factor in developing a vaccine. Gertrude Elion, one of the first women medical researchers to obtain an executive position with a major pharmaceutical firm, synthesized drugs to treat gout, leukemia, and organ transplant rejection. Gladys Anderson Emerson was the first to isolate vitamin E from wheat germ oil, and she conducted groundbreaking research into the relationship between cancer and nutrition.

Anatomist Bertha Vogel Scharrer codeveloped the theory of

hormonal neurosecretion, now a central tenet in physiology. Nobel Prize winner (1987) Rita Levi-Montalcini, an Italian neurobiologist, is best known for her codiscovery in 1954 of Nerve Growth Factor, a previously unknown biological mechanism that stimulates the growth of nerve cells.

Rebecca Lancefield is credited with first categorizing the organism responsible for rheumatic fever. Martha May Eliot, first woman president of the American Public Health Association, is credited with codeveloping the cure for rickets: plenty of sunshine and cod-liver oil. Dorothy Hansine Anderson was the first to identify cystic fibrosis, and she devised an easy method of diagnosing the disease in its early stages. And molecular biologist Karen Elizabeth Willard-Gallo invented and patented a method for early detection of infectious mononucleosis.

Gladys Hobby / Elizabeth McCoy / Dorothy Fennel / Dorothy Hodgkin / Margaret Hutchinson

PENICILLIN

The Second World War created two monumental, antithetical scientific projects. One was the race to develop an ultimate weapon of destruction: the nuclear bomb. The other was the race to develop the era's ultimate weapon against death: penicillin. Some remarkable—and remarkably overlooked—women made significant contributions to both inventions.

Without resorting to hyperbole, one can say that penicillin revolutionized medicine. It was the first safe antibiotic, the first germ-killer that also didn't kill the patient. Over the years it has proven to be effective against almost all bacteria harmful to man, and it is the standard treatment for diseases as diverse as anthrax, diphtheria, tetanus, pneumonia, cholera, typhoid poisoning, syphilis and gonorrhea, scarlet fever and other streptococcal infections, and septicemia.

"Penicillin," according to David Wilson, author of *In Search of Penicillin*, ". . . opened the way to our present society in which we positively expect the medical scientist to produce a cure for almost every disease by finding some chemical, drug, or other mode of treatment."

Like the atomic bomb, penicillin is not the responsibility of one individual. Sir Alexander Fleming, a British physician, discovered the unique antibacterial properties of penicillin molds in 1928, but he misunderstood their implication and never pursued their development. Ten years later, Howard Florey, an Australian physiologist, and Ernst Chain, a German biochemist—working together in England—came across Fleming's forgotten findings and developed the first crude penicillin drug.

Gladys Hobby, a microbiologist at Columbia University, read with interest a 1940 report of Florey and Chain's findings. Working with Dr. Martin Henry and biochemist Karl Meyer, Hobby began purifying the Florey-Chain prototype. Within five weeks, they became the first ever to treat a patient with penicillin injection; within six months they had cured a patient with the drug. The team then began producing the United States' first supply of penicillin.

Hobby went on to join the research division of Pfizer, Inc., where she developed Terramycin, an antibiotic more effective against some diseases than penicillin itself.

Also involved in the wartime effort to perfect penicillin were Drs. Dorothy I. Fennel and Elizabeth McCoy. Working at Northern Research Laboratory in 1942, Fennel was part of the team that was honored with the USDA Distinguished Service Team Award in 1947 for its development of a powerful new penicillin species. *Penicillium fennelliae* is named for its inventor. McCoy did similar work at the University of Wisconsin, where she discovered a high-yield penicillin that allowed the drug to be produced in large quantities during the war effort.

The early production of penicillin was a spit-and-baling-wire operation that utilized milk churns, aquarium pumps, and bands of loyal volunteers who stood in zero-temperature lockers and shook jars of culture fluid. Chemical engineer Margaret H. Hutchinson designed equipment and processes for purification and recovery that led to the construction of the first commercial penicillin plant. In 1955 she won the Society of Women Engineers Achievement Award.

Dr. Dorothy Crowfoot Hodgkin made possible the synthetic production (by artificial means) of penicillin by determining its molecular structure. Using complex X-ray crystallography, the British researcher completed her exacting seven-year project in 1949. In 1964 Hodgkin became the third woman to win the Nobel Prize for chemistry (joining Marie Curie and Irène Joliot-Curie) for her structural analyses of penicillin and, subsequently, vitamin B_{12}.

Louise Pearce

SLEEPING SICKNESS SERUM

Coinventor of the serum that cures sleeping sickness, Dr. Louise Pearce went alone in 1920 to the then-Belgian Congo to treat victims of the disease, which was ravaging Africa at the time. Her work both in the lab and in the field saved tens of thousands of lives, and she is largely responsible for eradicating sleeping sickness as a modern-day health problem.

Born in 1885, Louise Pearce was an outstanding student, graduating with a B.A. in physiology from Stanford in 1907 and an M.D. in 1909 from Johns Hopkins. One of the first career medical researchers, she joined a team at the Rockefeller Institute assigned to find a cure for the dreaded African disease, which inflames the brain and creates in its victims a constant state of drowsiness.

Contemporary researchers had isolated the cause of the disease: a microscopic parasite transmitted to humans by the bite of the tsetse fly. A cure, though, had eluded the medical establishment. Pearce and her partner, Wade Hampton Brown, began investigating the possibility that Salvarsan—an organic compound containing arsenic that had been used successfully in treating syphilis—might lead them to an anti-sleeping sickness agent.

The quest bore fruit in 1919, when the pair isolated a compound, later known as "tryparsamide," which effectively destroyed the disease in test animals. Anxious to put the drug into use, Pearce traveled to Leopoldville in the Belgian Congo, where she conducted a scientifically planned program to determine tryparsamide's efficacy. Within weeks, even victims with the most severe cases of sleeping sickness were cured and the effects of their illness reversed.

The Belgian government was so grateful to Pearce that it honored her with the Order of the Crown of Belgium in 1920, and in 1953 it awarded her the King Leopold II Prize—a check for $10,000.

Hattie Elizabeth Alexander

MENINGITIS SERUM

When Hattie Alexander began researching influenza meningitis in the 1930s, the disease was 100 percent fatal in infants, and the treatment for adults was almost useless. Two years after she developed an antibody, deaths from the disease fell by 80 percent, and soon to only a tenth of the former numbers.

Meningococcal disease, which afflicts mostly children between three months and adolescence, is an inflammation of the meninges, the membranes surrounding the brain and the spinal cord. Each year some twenty-five hundred people in the United States are stricken with the disease. Despite the Alexander antibody, ten to 20 percent of the severe cases are misdiagnosed and untreated, and continue to be fatal. Occasionally, less than ten hours elapse from the onset of symptoms to death.

The woman who found a cure for this common infant-killer grew up in a family of eight children in Baltimore. A bright student in high school, she won a scholarship to Goucher College, where she performed adequately if not spectacularly. It was her work for three years after college at the Maryland and U.S. Public Health services that convinced Johns Hopkins University officials to allow her to enter their medical school and that also first piqued her interest in bacteriology.

She established an outstanding record at medical school, and she interned at Columbia-Presbyterian Medical Center Babies' Hospital, where she witnessed the casualties of influenza meningitis almost daily. Working with an immunochemist named Michael Heidelberger, she labored for several years without success in attempting to find a cure for the disease. Ultimately it was her background as a bacteriologist as well as a medical doctor that allowed her to isolate an antibody and then develop an antiserum.

World-renowned for her discovery, Dr. Alexander went on to contribute significant research in bacterial genetics. She was among the first to demonstrate the validity of a new theory that stated DNA influences genetic characteristics.

As director of Columbia-Presbyterian Medical Center's microbiological laboratory, she was known as an innovative teacher with a dislike for lectures and an ability to maximize the potential of students. She was one of the first women to head a national medical society when appointed president of the American Pediatrics Society. Dr. Alexander died of cancer in 1968.

Anna Wessel Williams

DIPHTHERIA IMMUNIZATION; RABIES VACCINATION

A pioneer in pathology—the study of the nature of disease—Anna Wessel Williams saved thousands of lives by virtually eliminating diphtheria in the Western world and by controlling rabies.

Born during the Civil War, Anna was taught at home by her parents, and for two years was a teacher herself. When her younger sister almost died delivering a stillborn child, Anna made the decision to devote her life to medicine, despite the objections of her mother. Anna obtained an M.D. from the Women's Medical College of New York in 1891 and eventually took a post at the newly created diagnostic lab of the city's health department—the first of its kind in the country.

The lab's first priority was to stop the diphtheria epidemic raging through the city at the time. Severely contagious, the disease derives its name from the Greek word for leather, *diphthera,* because sufferers form a tough, yellowish-gray membrane in their throats. The toxin of the diphtheria germ causes inflammation in the heart and nervous system and was a leading killer of children.

A diphtheria antitoxin had been developed, but it was too weak to be effective and impossible to manufacture in the massive quantities needed. Williams isolated an unusually strong and prolific strain, which bears her name and remains in production today. Her discovery turned the tide against the epidemic, and the antitoxin made diphtheria a rare disease in most of the world.

Having conquered diphtheria, Williams turned her attention to rabies. By 1896 the Pasteur Institute in Paris had isolated the first effective rabies antitoxin, and Williams was the first American physician to travel to Europe to obtain a culture of the virus. Through her efforts enough vaccine was obtained to begin large-scale production in the United States in 1898.

Even with a rabies vaccine available, many bite victims were still dying because it took so long to diagnose whether the animal itself was rabid. Concurrently with an Italian physician named Adelchi Negri, Williams identified the distinctive brain cell peculiar to an animal with rabies. She went on to invent a method that quickly detected the "Negri bodies," a method still in use today. The first woman to chair the lab section of the American Public Health Association, Williams died in 1954 at age ninety-one.

Elizabeth Hazen / Rachel Brown

NYSTATIN

Since its discovery in 1948 by Elizabeth Hazen and Rachel Brown, the antibiotic nystatin—the first safe fungicide—has been used effectively for everything from curing athlete's foot to restoring paintings and books.

Nystatin was the greatest biomedical breakthrough since the 1928 discovery of penicillin. Penicillin was the first antibiotic proven to be a safe and effective treatment in humans against disease-producing bacteria; nystatin was its counterpart against disease-producing fungi. The development of nystatin initiated cures for a variety of afflictions, from ringworm to life-threatening diseases.

Even today, untreated fungal diseases in the developed nations kill some seven hundred people annually . . . more than meningitis, syphilis, and rheumatic fever combined.

Aside from its therapeutic uses for human beings, nystatin has found many other applications. Horticulturists use it as an effective treatment against Dutch elm disease. The food and livestock industries use it in combating molds. Even the art world has gotten into the picture. When the Arno River in Florence overflowed its banks in 1966, nystatin was used to stop the growth of fungus that threatened to destroy priceless art treasures damaged by the floodwaters.

The nystatin discoverers came from disparate but equally disadvantaged backgrounds. Born in 1885 in rural Mississippi, Hazen was two years old when her father died; her mother died the following year. Raised by her uncle and aunt, she financed her graduate studies in microbiology at Columbia University by working for six years as a public-school teacher.

Brown was born in 1898 in Springfield, Massachusetts. Her father abandoned the family when she was twelve years old; her mother became the sole breadwinner not only for Rachel and her brother but for her grandparents as well. Rachel had little hope of attending college until a wealthy matron, a friend of the family, intervened and financed her education.

When Brown met her future collaborator in 1948, Hazen was considered one of the leading authorities in the identification of fungus. Brown's job as the chemist was to isolate the antitoxin agent. Within a year, they had found and separated the antifungal substance in a soil sample that Hazen had collected from a friend's farm in Virginia.

After announcing their discovery in 1950, Hazen and Brown were wooed by every major pharmaceutical house in the country with lucrative offers to produce the fungicide. Instead, the duo patented the drug through a nonprofit research corporation. The fund generated $13 million in research grants, playing a key role in mycology for thirty years. The women refused any share of the royalties from their invention, and they continued to live on civil servants' salaries until their deaths. Asked why she refused to enjoy some of the wealth she and Hazen had earned, Brown replied simply, "If you have enough, why should you want more?"

Florence Seibert

DISTILLED WATER APPARATUS; PURE TUBERCULIN

A pioneering chemist in the diagnosis and treatment of tuberculosis, Florence Seibert was that rare combination of pure scientist and practical inventor.

Born in 1897 in Easton, Pennsylvania, Florence contracted infantile paralysis at age three and was left severely lame. When a professor advised that she might be physically inadequate to be a physician, she reluctantly switched from her first love of medicine to chemistry, obtaining her Ph.D. from Yale in 1923. Yet Florence rarely considered herself "handicapped," saying she was often shocked when she encountered her own reflection. "That's the only time I ever seem able to remember [my paralysis]. And even in my forties, I'm still brought up with a jolt every time I get in front of a mirror and see myself coming," she once said.

Following graduation, she joined a research team in Chicago attempting to refine tuberculin, the substance used to detect tuberculosis. Simultaneously, she became interested in a phenomenon that had baffled physicians. In certain surgical procedures, distilled water is injected into patients. Yet even when the water was sterilized three times, it sometimes produced life-threatening fevers in the patients; no one knew why.

Calling upon her biochemical background, Seibert deduced

126

that bacterial chemicals, which remained in the water even after distillation, were the culprits. Sterilization killed the bacteria, but traces of toxic chemicals they left behind were entering the water via steam droplets produced in distillation. Dr. Seibert solved the whole problem by designing a trap for the steam droplets in the still, thereby making multiple distillations unnecessary.

Dr. Seibert accomplished this during her first year on the job, then turned her attention back to the task of finding a pure form of tuberculin. Robert Koch had discovered the causative microorganism of tuberculosis in 1882. By growing the tubercle bacilli in beef broth, Koch concocted the first tuberculin, a nonlethal derivative of the germ that, injected under the skin, gave a positive test reaction for tuberculosis. The only problem with Koch's tuberculin was that it was extremely impure and therefore often an unreliable test.

After eight years of research, Dr. Seibert isolated the active tuberculin protein by inventing a special filter. Her substance, purified protein derivative, is the international standard for the manufacture of tuberculin, and a test for its purity.

Although tuberculosis no longer afflicts the industrialized world in epidemic proportions, "the great white plague" was the leading cause of death in the United States as late as 1911. While deaths attributed to tuberculosis in North America have dropped below three thousand annually, it remains today a virulent killer in the Third World, with mortality rates fluctuating between six and nine times that of North America.

Alice Evans

BRUCELLOSIS

In 1917 U.S. government health researcher Alice Evans announced that she had discovered the cause of a deadly disease. No one believed her.

As described by a prominent scientist, brucellosis was "common throughout the world, insidious in onset, difficult to diagnose, and marked by recurrent bouts of fever and malaise. It has ruined the productive lives of many persons and is one of the most miserable diseases of man." It was also thought to be several different diseases, some of them afflicting livestock as well as humans. In cows it was called Bang's disease; in goats, Malta fever. In man it often fell under the descriptive but imprecise name of "undulant fever" because of recurring high temperatures accompanying the infection.

When Evans discovered that all these maladies were caused by a single organism, she already had seven years' experience as a researcher in dairy studies for various departments of the U.S. government. Yet her announcement was greeted with howls of disbelief by the established scientific community: If indeed all these diseases had a common cause, surely someone would have discovered that by now.

When she coupled her announcement of the cause of "undulant fever" with its remedy—the pasteurization of milk—the entire dairy industry joined in the attack. For nearly a decade, Evans's findings would be largely ignored, although she never gave up the fight.

128

By the turn of the century, medical researchers had traced the source of "undulant fever" to milk, but the cause of the contamination remained a mystery. The cattle from which the contaminated milk had been obtained appeared healthy, so the prevailing thought was that the milk was somehow contaminated after it left the cow. Compounding the confusion was that the milk identified as causing undulant fever was not spoiled; it smelled and tasted fresh. Thus pasteurization—the heat treatment process invented by Louis Pasteur in the 1860s and used primarily for stopping spoilage in beer and wine—was rejected as a solution.

Unknown at the time was the fact that the microbes of the brucellosis bred especially well in the udders of lactating cows and that healthy-looking cows could produce infected milk for months and even years before succumbing to the disease. The heat in the pasteurization process offered a relatively simple solution to killing the brucellosis microbes, but the dairy industry was not equipped for pasteurization and resisted the capital expenditures it would require.

When Evans suggested that the cow, not the milk, might be the source of the problem, her theory was resoundingly rejected by her bureaucratic superiors, who ordered lab tests restricted to milk already known to be contaminated. Alice secretly conducted her own tests of fresh milk drawn directly from the udder, which led to her discovery of the origins of brucellosis.

By comparing various cultures of other livestock-transmitted diseases that produced similar symptoms in humans, she established that the various microorganisms were related and in fact constituted a whole new genus. In the course of her research, she was accidentally infected with a rare form of brucellosis in 1922 and would suffer recurring bouts of the disease for the next two decades.

By the late 1920s, other scientists had confirmed Evans's theory. In 1928 the Society of American Bacteriologists elected her its first woman president. By the 1930s even the intransigent dairy industry came around and adopted pasteurization as a standard practice, dramatically reducing the outbreak of "undulant fever."

Once asked why the leading microbiologist of the time had

129

rejected her findings on brucellosis, she replied: "The Nineteenth Amendment was not a part of the constitution of the United States when the controversy began, and he was not accustomed to considering a scientific idea proposed by a woman."

Rosalyn Yalow

RADIOIMMUNOASSAY

In 1977 Rosalyn Yalow won the Nobel Prize for her invention of a medical tool called radioimmunoassay. She became the second woman ever to win the coveted prize for medicine, and the sixth woman to win in any science category over the seventy-seven-year history of the award.

In awarding the prize, the Nobel Committee described Yalow's technique as having "brought about a revolution in biological and medical research." Basically a way to measure minute substances in the body by using radioactive particles as tracers, radioimmunoassay (RIA) has indeed revolutionized medical diagnosis, more than any discovery since the X ray.

The beauty of the technique is that it is not limited to one specialty of medicine, nor even to the field of medicine alone. RIA today is used to measure hormones, vitamins, enzymes, toxins, and other substances that, prior to this invention, were too minute for physicians to detect. Doctors use RIA to diagnose diabetes, thyroid disease, hypertension, sterility, and even some forms of cancer. Blood banks can use it to test their inventory for hepatitis. Criminologists have used it to detect the presence of a lethal drug in corpses.

In accepting her Nobel Prize in 1977, Dr. Yalow spoke of the need for more women scientists: "We must believe in ourselves or no one else will believe in us," she said. This has been her credo since a childhood during the Great Depression, as the second child of working-class, first-generation Jewish immigrants. Her father ran a paper and twine business, and her mother took in sewing to help make ends meet. Neither parent ever attended high school.

When Rosalyn needed braces on her teeth, she had to earn the money for them by helping with the sewing. But although her parents were unable to provide much more than basic food and shelter, they did instill in their daughter the idea that she could accomplish anything she set her mind to. "I never really got the message that girls were not as important as boys. I was very close to my father. He took me to baseball games. I can tell you all about the 1934 Yankee team!" she said with a laugh.

Having decided she wanted to be a scientist by age eight, Rosalyn graduated from Hunter College at age nineteen, receiving a degree in chemistry and physics in 1941. Unable to secure a graduate school assistantship (one midwestern school flatly stated that the chances of a Jewish female finding a job in physics were nil), she agreed to take a secretarial position with a Columbia University biochemist. "The idea was if I was a good girl, I could take a course there," she recalled.

World politics intervened. Shortly after World War II was declared, the University of Illinois notified Rosalyn that her application had been accepted after all. The war, it seems, had depleted the ranks of male graduate students. Rosalyn became the first woman admitted to the University of Illinois physics department as a graduate assistant since 1917.

Receiving her doctorate in 1945, Yalow began her work in nuclear medicine in 1947. She joined a Veterans Administration hospital in the Bronx as a part-time consultant in radioisotopes, an advanced medical tool only recently available in quantity. Anxious to participate in the medical revolution that radioisotopes promised, Dr. Yalow converted a janitor's closet at the hospital into a makeshift laboratory. Since commercial equipment was unavailable, she constructed and designed her own apparatus to measure the radioactive material, and she conducted eight research projects with various physicians over the next five years.

In 1950 she joined forces with Dr. Solomon A. Berson, a young internist, who codeveloped the RIA technique with her. A perfect complement to one another's talents, their partnership lasted twenty-two years, until Dr. Berson's untimely death from a heart attack. Dr. Berson would have shared the Nobel with Yalow, but the prize is never given posthumously.

Devasted by the loss of her workmate, Dr. Yalow named her lab for him; however, she did find new collaborators in the search for knowledge. She was honored in 1976 with the prestigious Albert Lasker Basic Medical Research Award, the first woman to receive it. She would receive half a dozen other important accolades before topping it all with the Nobel Prize.

Rosalyn and her husband, Aaron Yalow—a noted physics professor—raised two children, each of whom pursued a professional career. Never accepting the notion that she would have to sacrifice motherhood for science, or vice versa, Dr. Yalow was once quoted as saying, "We still live in a world in which a significant fraction of people, including women, believe that a woman belongs—and wants to belong—exclusively in the home. . . . The world cannot afford the loss of the talents of half of its people if we are to solve the many problems which beset us."

Dr. Virginia Apgar

THE APGAR SCORE

"Every baby born in a modern hospital anywhere in the world is looked at first through the eyes of Virginia Apgar," a noted physician once remarked. Dr. Apgar invented the classic Newborn Scoring System, commonly called the Apgar Score, which since 1952 has saved the lives of innumerable newborns. Prior to the Apgar Score, physicians had no way of determining the health of a baby in the first crucial minutes after its birth.

Born in 1909, Viriginia Apgar pursued a medical degree at Columbia University, and she became one of the first women graduates of its medical school, in 1933. She also became one of the first women to specialize in surgery, and she began a prestigious internship at Columbia-Presbyterian Medical Center.

Despite several hundred successful operations, Dr. Apgar became convinced after two years that she would never be able to reach her full potential as a surgeon because of her gender. And she placed as much of the blame on women as on men: "Women won't go to a woman surgeon. Only the Lord can answer that one," she said with a sigh.

She turned instead to anesthesiology, which she almost single-handedly established as a separate medical discipline. The practice of anesthesiology, long dominated by women—that is, nurses—was in dire need of more sophisticated medical specialists. Beginning in 1938, Dr. Apgar served for eleven years as director of anesthesiology at Columbia-Presbyterian Medical Center, creating an entirely new academic department. In 1949 the university appointed her its first full professor of anesthesiology, thereby recognizing the field as a separate medical discipline for the first time anywhere.

At the height of her career as a medical administrator, she returned to research to study anesthesia and childbirth. In 1952 she introduced the Apgar Score, which measures five crucial aspects of a newborn's health: pulse, respiration, muscle tone, color, and reflexes.

As Apgar herself wrote in her book *Is My Baby All Right?*: "Birth is the most hazardous time of life. . . . It's urgently important to evaluate quickly the status of a just-born baby and to identify immediately those who need emergency care."

Many infants die because of undetected prenatal problems that become aggravated after birth or because of injuries that occur during the trauma of birth, such as brain hemorrhaging or asphyxia or a combination of these factors.

Before the universal application of the Apgar Score, newborns were simply wrapped in a blanket and examined later in the nursery. Respiratory and circulatory problems, which if detected immediately after birth could have been corrected easily, were often fatal.

After assisting in some seventeen thousand births, Apgar moved on to still another career. In 1959 she agreed to become director of research of the National Foundation-March of Dimes, where she conducted important work in preventing birth defects. In addition to her work as a scientist, she was an indefatigable fundraiser, increasing the foundation's annual income from $19 million when she began to $46 million at the time of her death in 1974. Never married, the quick-witted Apgar once explained: "It's just that I haven't found a man who can cook."

Sara Josephine Baker

EYEDROPPER AND INFANT
CLOTHING

In a career that spanned the four turbulent decades between the Gay Nineties and World War II, Sara Josephine Baker embodied the I-can-do-anything spirit of the emerging American "new woman." In her various roles as city administrator, world statesman, suffragette, physician, and journalist, she encounterd a cast of characters that included everyone from Lillian Russell to Typhoid Mary. But her lasting legacy and the inspiration for her inventions was Dr. Baker's pioneering work in child health care.

The programs she established as a New York City health administrator were adopted internationally, as were her designs for the first modern-day infant wear and for an eyedropper that virtually eliminated congenital blindness.

Born in 1873 to a genteel family in Poughkeepsie, New York, Josephine remembers a steady stream of weekend visitors from that "new fangled" women's school nearby, Vassar College. Some of the young women were studying science, but Josephine was too busy with her own schooling to take much interest.

"I was thoroughly trained in the business of being a woman [with] a rigorous education in cooking and sewing," she wrote in her autobiography, *Fighting for Life*. "I was reared in a thoroughly conventional tradition and took to it happily. I understood that after I left school I would go to Vassar, and then, I supposed, I would get married and raise a family and that would be that."

Her life was irrevocably changed when her brother and then her father died when she was sixteen, the latter of typhoid fever. The family could no longer afford to send Josephine to Vassar, so she began looking for a profession in which to earn a living. Although she never broaches the subject in her book, her father's death must have been instrumental in the decision to devote her life to medicine—despite strenuous protests from her mother, friends, and even the family physician.

Still, Josephine never approached the medical profession as a starry-eyed idealist. "I was not quite eighteen, but quite old enough to worry over the time and money I might be wasting if I did not succeed. . . . Only the chorus of I-told-you-so's that would have greeted me kept me from dropping it all and going home," she said.

Receiving her degree in 1898 (second in a class of eighteen) from the Women's Medical College in New York, Dr. Baker hung up her shingle as a general practitioner and waited for the clients to pour in. It was more like a trickle. In her first year of private practice, she earned only $185—although at least one iconoclastic woman patient quite liked the idea of a female physician. "One day I was sent up to West End Avenue to examine a client and much to my surprise met Lillian Russell. She was the loveliest, most natural, and most charming person I had ever seen. It was one of my first red-letter days."

In 1901 Dr. Baker secured a position as a medical inspector for the city, a position that paid twice what she was earning in private practice. The Tammany Hall politicos who ran the city health department were no more enlightened than anyone else at the time when it came to hiring women physicians, but the job was hardly a plum. Dr. Baker's beat was Hell's Kitchen, one of the worst ghetto areas in the country.

Working alone, her job was to go from tenement to tenement, inspecting for contagious diseases such as dysentery, smallpox, influenza, and typhoid fever, which were ravaging the immigrant population. "This time I had let myself in for a really grueling ordeal. In my district, the heart of old Hell's Kitchen on the West Side, the heat, the smells, the squalor made it something not to be believed. I climbed stair after stair, knocked on door after door, met drunk after drunk, filthy mother after filthy mother and dying baby after dying baby," Dr. Baker recalled.

This experience hardened her attitude ("I had a sincere conviction that they would all be better off dead than so degradingly alive") but strengthened her resolve. She was appointed assistant health commissioner because of her exemplary field work, which included tracking down infamous typhoid carrier "Typhoid Mary" Mallon. (An Irish immigrant with no family, Typhoid Mary earned her livelihood as a cook and was responsible for at least ten outbreaks of the dreaded disease as she moved from one household to the next, infecting all those whom she fed. Never stricken with the disease herself, Mallon refused to believe she was a carrier. Baker actually apprehended her twice. After being released the first time upon assurances to health authorities that she would not work as a cook, Mallon was found a second time, working in a hospital kitchen. Typhoid Mary died, still in custody, in 1938.)

In spite of the hardships Dr. Baker encountered because she was a woman—her all-male staff resigned en masse upon her appointment—the attractive doctor quickly became a shrewd and effective bureaucrat. She not only cajoled her staff to return, but also coerced the city fathers into establishing the world's first tax-supported child hygiene department.

Her first goal was to tackle the appalling infant mortality total in New York's squalid slums, which was as high as fifteen hundred per week. From what she had witnessed, she determined that many of the deaths were caused by pure ignorance. "The way to keep people from dying from disease, it struck me suddenly, was to keep them from falling ill. Healthy people didn't die. It sounds like a completely witless remark, but at that time it was a startling idea. Preventative medicine had hardly been born yet and had no promotion in public health work."

With a team of thirty nurses, Dr. Baker went door-to-door teaching young mothers the basics of nutrition, cleanliness, and proper ventilation. She established "milk stations" where free pasteurized milk was distributed, and she devised a simple baby formula of lime water and milk sugar that any mother could make at home. She created the "Little Mother's League" to teach baby care to children left in charge of their siblings. She licensed midwives, and she standardized inspections of schoolchildren for contagious diseases.

When she learned that the restrictive infant wear of the day had actually strangled some babies, she found herself "turning couturiere and designing an entirely new system of baby clothes," inventing the "obvious, but previously unthought-of, system of making baby clothes all open down the front." Her designs were copied by McCall's Pattern Company, and Metropolitan Life Insurance Company distributed two hundred thousand of the patterns to their policyholders.

Similarly, she set out to halt the needless blinding of infants caused by improper administration of the eyedrops that all babies received to prevent gonorrheal infection. The 1 percent silver nitrate solution used was usually stored in bottles where it could become contaminated, and often it evaporated to dangerously high concentration. Dr. Baker invented a foolproof, sanitary packing solution utilizing two beeswax capsules, each containing enough solution for one eye. The method was adopted worldwide.

Her programs decreased the infant mortality rate from fifteen hundred a week to three hundred in the slum area where they were tested, and within fifteen years New York could claim the lowest infant mortality rate of any city in America or Europe. Determined that child hygiene should become a national priority, Dr. Baker agreed to retire in 1923 only after all forty-eight states initiated similar programs. She also oversaw the establishment of the Federal Children's Bureau and Public Health Service, the forerunner of today's Department of Health and Human Services.

Her retirement was anything but leisurely. From 1922 to 1924 she represented the United States on the Health Committee of the League of Nations. Between 1935 and 1936 she served as president of the American Medical Women's Association.

Aside from her work in health care, Dr. Baker was a noted political activist. A reluctant feminist at first, she found herself drawn into "the great struggle to get political recognition of the fact that women are as much human beings as men are." One particular incident convinced her of the need for reform. Although invited to lecture at New York University Medical School in 1916, she was denied the opportunity to earn its new doctorate of public health because she was a woman. She broke this sex barrier and went on to become an articulate speaker for the movement, doing her share of soapbox oration for the largely male lunchtime crowd in New York City. She was a member of the suffragette delegation that visited Woodrow Wilson at the White House and received his official endorsement of the Nineteenth Amendment.

Author of three books and some 250 articles, Dr. Baker continued working from her home in rural New Jersey until shortly before her death in 1945. Never married, she once wrote of her career, "I believe that this salvaging of human life has been worthwhile. I can still see the light in a mother's eye when her baby was assured of health."

Helen Brooke Taussig

''BLUE BABY OPERATION''

Helen Taussig is best known as the codeveloper of the operation to save "blue babies"—their condition was a leading cause of infant death before the 1940s—but she also conducted important research in rheumatic fever and was the first U.S. physician to warn of the impending danger of Thalidomide.

Born in 1898, Taussig did not enter the field of medicine until after taking an undergraduate degree from Berkeley in 1921. On a suggestion from her father, she applied to the Harvard School of Public Health, only to be informed that she could study there but not be awarded a degree because she was a woman.

Ironically, this first encounter with sex discrimination cemented her resolve to enter the medical profession. She accepted the offer at Harvard, determined to break the barriers that kept women out. She endured for a while, attending lectures on the condition that she sat in a corner by herself, and could only examine tissue culture slides in a separate room. When denied permission to study anatomy altogether, she transferred to Boston University.

Despite a stellar performance at Boston University, the dean of the medical school—realizing she was serious about completing her degree—suggested that she move to Johns Hopkins, which by then had a twenty-year history of "tolerating" women students. Transferring to that university, Taussig at last thought she had found a safe harbor from prejudice. Upon graduating, though, she was informed that she could not intern at Johns Hopkins in her chosen speciality of internal medicine because the department already had one woman intern.

Switching to pediatrics, Taussig won a fellowship with the university's cardiac clinic and began studying congenital heart malformation. For eleven years she served as head of the children's cardiac clinic, where she encountered dozens of cases of the condition known as "blue baby" or pulmonary stenosis, which frequently resulted in death or brain damage. Medical scientists knew that the babies were born with blue-tinged skin because of a shortage of oxygen in the blood, but no one had discovered why the condition occurred or how to correct it.

Dr. Taussig's research pointed to the fact that blue babies had a malformed pulmonary artery, the vessel that carries blood from the heart to the lungs and supplies it with fresh oxygen. If a bypass could be constructed from the heart to the lung, then . . . "Not being a surgeon," she said, "it gave me no difficulty to ask, if you can tie off a ductus, why can't you build a new one altogether?"

She had to wait until 1941, when a pioneer heart surgeon named Dr. Alfred Blalock arrived at Johns Hopkins, before she could find a colleague to attempt so daring a technique. Convinced of the soundness of her theory, he began experimenting on animals with the method she described. In 1944, after two years of testing, he performed the first successful "blue baby" operation, which thereafter became known as the Blalock-Taussig Method.

Beyond its immediate benefit, the Blalock-Taussig Method demonstrated that even newborns with congenital defects could survive heart surgery, thus opening the door to the development of other cardiac operations. Although her partner initially received most of the recognition, Dr. Taussig went on to be awarded a bevy of honors, including the U.S. Medal of Freedom, France's Chevalier Légion d'Honneur, and—perhaps most satisfying of all—an honorary degree from Boston University.

Not content to rest on her laurels, Taussig pursued her work in congenital heart disease and became the first woman president of the American Heart Association. But it was her work as a pediatrics professor at Johns Hopkins that, inadvertently, brought her into the national limelight again.

In 1962 one of her students, a German doctor, mentioned that an unusually large number of grossly deformed babies were being born in Europe. Troubled by the phenomenon, Taussig, then sixty-four, immediately flew to Europe, where she visited pediatrics clinics in Germany and England. Convinced that a recently introduced sleeping pill, Thalidomide, was the common factor among mothers of the deformed babies, Taussig returned to the United States and was the first physician to warn the medical community of the drug's danger.

Taussig's caveat confirmed the long-held suspicions of Dr. Frances Kelsey, a medical officer with the U.S. Food and Drug Administration, that the drug caused birth defects. The drug was never allowed to enter the U.S. market, although by the time it was removed from the world market in 1962, some ten thousand "Thalidomide babies" had been born.

Dr. Helen Brooke Taussig died in 1986 at age eighty-eight, as a result of injuries suffered in a Pennsylvania car crash.

The Nuclear Club

CONSIDERING THAT THE ENTIRE DISCIPLINE was founded by Marie Curie, it's only natural that many women have gravitated toward the study of atomic energy. What is unnatural is the recognition, or lack thereof, they have received for their efforts.

History credits Enrico Fermi with first producing nuclear fission; in fact, Fermi first *fused* uranium nuclei, and it was Lise Meitner who split them. Evidence further suggests that Irène Joliot-Curie had identified the phenomenon of nuclear fission even earlier than Meitner but hid its terrible secrets from the world. She feared it would be used as a weapon of war—and she was right. A number of women were active participants in the infamous Manhattan Project and continue to excel in the field of atomic physics to this day.

More women than there is room to detail have made major

contributions in the field of nuclear science and invention. Worthy of note in atomic energy are Margaret Butler, a fellow of the American Nuclear Society and a mathematician who combines the sciences of atomics and computers; Hatice Sadan Cullingford, coinventor of the apparatus that stores hydrogen isotopes; and Dorothy Martin Simon, the first to isolate an isotope of calcium. Ann Savolainen was the first female member of the American Nuclear Society; Louisa Fernandez Hansen is a senior physicist at Lawrence Livermore Laboratory; Nina Byers serves the European Organization for Nuclear Research; and Kristen Johnson has pioneered the use of the cyclotron in treating human cancer.

The Curies

RADIOACTIVITY

Marie Curie is generally labeled "scientist" rather than "inventor" because her brilliance as the former tends to overshadow her accomplishments as the latter. Yet in 1898 she invented a new chemical process for extracting radioactive material from ore, a technique she could have patented but that she viewed only as a tool for unlocking the secrets of radioactivity. She also invented the prototype radiation counter that today bears the name of German physicist Hans Geiger. Less known is that Marie's daughter Irène won the Nobel Prize in 1935 for coinventing (with her husband) a method for creating artificial radioactive elements.

Widely accepted as the greatest woman scientist of all time, Marie Curie is the only person ever to win two Nobel Prizes, an accomplishment made even sweeter by the fact that they were in different disciplines. Her discovery of radium—the first material capable of emitting light and heat with no appreciable transformation—and her subsequent development of the concept of radioactivity ushered in the atomic age.

"No one single discovery, not even Pasteur's far-reaching discovery of microbic life, it may safely be asserted, has ever been more subversive of long-accepted views in certain domains of science, or given rise to more perplexing problems regarding matters which were previously thought to be thoroughly understood," wrote H. J. Mozans, author of the first comprehensive book on women in science, in 1913. His assessment of her significance to science is limited only by his inability to foresee how her research would forever change the way we live.

Her intellect was—excuse the pun—radiant, affecting those closest to her the most. Aside from her Nobel Prize–winning daughter and son-in-law, Frédéric Joliot (who was Marie's lab assistant when Irène met him), another of Marie's lab assistants, Marguérite Perey, disovered the eighty-seventh element (francium) and became a noted nuclear physicist.

The public Marie Curie was a saintly figure, a woman who put her sister through medical school before beginning her own research, who subsisted on milk and bread for three years while completing her university studies, who endured the premature death of her beloved husband and gloriously carried on their work, who risked her life during World War I helping the wounded on the front lines, and who eventually and quite literally died for science, from exposure to radiation. Poor for most of her professional life, she could have profited handsomely from her process of isolating radium, the discovery that earned her the unprecedented second Nobel Prize. (In 1920 one gram of radium was valued at $100,000.) "It would be contrary to the scientific spirit," she said of profit-taking.

Marie Curie's presence was so stellar that, ironically, she may have inadvertently hindered the development of other women in science: 'Before long most professors and department chairmen were . . . expecting every female aspirant for a faculty position to be a Marie Curie," writes Margaret Rossiter, author of *Women*

Scientists in America. "They routinely compared American women scientists of all ages to Curie and, finding them wanting, justified not hiring them on the unreasonable grounds that they were not as good as she, twice a Nobel Laureate!"

Born in 1867 in Poland, Marie Sklodowska was a precocious child who taught herself to read by the time she was four. Her father, a chemistry professor, introduced her into the lab at an early age; she was the only assistant he could afford. Her decision to postpone her university studies appears to have been a combination of, first, her desire to finance her elder sister's education and second, the need to recover from a broken love affair. In any event, she worked as a governess for six years.

She arrived in Paris in 1891 with fifty francs in her pocket. After three years of living on ten cents a day, she graduated from the Sorbonne—the first woman ever admitted—with a degree in physical sciences (first in her class) and, one year later, an additional degree in mathematics (second in her class). She began working as a poorly paid assistant to a French physicist. Immediately recoizing her acumen, Professor Gabriel Lippman elevated her within a week to a full research position. Through her new circle of colleagues, she met Pierre Curie, already a lauded physical chemist. "What a great thing it would be," he once wrote to Marie, "to unite our lives and work together for the sake of science and humanity." This was precisely what they did for eleven years, from their marriage in 1895 to Pierre's death in 1906, when he was ignominiously run over by a truck.

Her research into radioactivity began in 1897, a year after French physicist Antoine Henri Becquerel had noticed that pitchblende (the ore uranium is extracted from) was spontaneously emitting rays that could not be accounted for by the mere presence of uranium. She quite correctly deduced that other elements, far more radioactive than uranium, were present in pitchblende, and she set out to isolate them. Pierre abandoned his celebrated studies on magnetism to assist his wife in her research.

Devising a new chemical method, she extracted a previously unknown element from pitchblende that she dubbed polonium, in honor of her native country. In that same year, 1898, she discovered radium. The scientific community at the time refused to believe the findings of the Curies, and the couple wasted years just extracting enough of the substance to continue their experiments. Shortly before the publication of her scientific paper on the phenomenon she called radioactivity, Marie received her first Nobel Prize (in physics), which she shared with Pierre and Becquerel. Pierre was also offered France's Legion of Honor, but he refused it because it was not awarded jointly with his wife.

During these years, Marie had two daughters: Irène, born 1897, and, Eve, born in 1904, who would eventually write her mother's biography. Pierre's death was devastating to Mme. Curie—in eleven years, they had never been separated for even a day. She became even more focused on her work: "I don't know whether, even by writing scientific books, I could live without the laboratory." Ascending to Pierre's professorship in 1906, she became the first woman teacher at the Sorbonne. In 1911 she was awarded the Nobel Prize in chemistry for isolating pure radium.

During World War I, with the assistance of her daughter Irène, Marie rushed to perfect the new medical diagnostic tool "X radiography." She learned to drive, acquainted herself with auto mechanics, and often would traverse rough terrain within the sounds of battle to install personally mobile X-ray equipment that served as many as one million soldiers.

Over the next two decades, she saw many of her dreams realized. The Curie Foundation for Research in Radioactivity was established in Paris, as well as the Radium Institute for Applied Medical Research in Warsaw—the latter headed by the sister whose medical education Marie had financed.

Her hands scarred and her hair falling out in patches from her years of exposure to radiation, Marie Curie died in 1934. One year later, her daughter Irène and her son-in-law would win the Nobel Prize in chemistry.

Born the year her mother began to study radioactivity, Irène's life seemed destined to be intertwined with her mother's. A brilliant scientist in her own right, Irène took an active interest in politics, the arts, and sports. She was raised largely by her grandfather, a doctor, and adopted his socialist ideology, which would figure importantly later in her life.

146

In 1918 she joined her mother at the Radium Institute. In 1925 she received her Ph.D. and met her future husband, Frédéric Joliot, a gifted young engineering student who also had become an assistant in Marie's lab. One year later they were married.

Their Nobel Prize–winning work involved bombarding various elements with alpha particles, artificially producing radioactive elements. A few years later Enrico Fermi would utilize their methodology to bombard uranium with neutrons, leading the way to Lise Meitner's discovery of atomic fission. Although best known for her collaborative work with Frédéric, Irène was noted as well for her independent research on the radioelements, including a doctoral thesis on alpha rays.

Irène adopted her mother's attitude about scientific inquiries and published all of her findings. However, in 1939, with the Nazi menace getting nearer, the couple ceased publication. The plans they had drawn for building a nuclear reactor were sealed in an envelope and secretly deposited with the French Academy of Science. The documents would not be uncovered for ten years, but later were instrumental in the construction of the first French nuclear reactor in 1948, thus ending the American-British monopoly.

Joining France's Socialist Party in 1934, the Joliot-Curies (this was Frédéric's legal surname after marriage, as well as Irène's) lent their support and prestige to Republican Spain during that country's Civil War. Irène even served in the Popular Front government in 1936. During Nazi occupation, they worked in protecting French scientists who were subject to imprisonment and sometimes execution. In 1944 Irène was forced to flee to Switzerland with their children.

In 1946 she was appointed director of the Radium Institute and was made a member of the French Atomic Energy Commission. She was removed from the commission in 1950, however, when she refused to denounce the Communist Party. Thereafter she and her husband devoted themselves to the laboratory. In 1955 she designed a new nuclear physics center and particle accelerator, which eventually would be constructed at the University of Orsay in 1958.

Her fate again paralleling her mother's, Irène died in 1956 in the Curie Hospital of leukemia caused by overexposure to radioactive material. As Marie had replaced Pierre at the Sorbonne, so Frédéric accepted Irène's professorship at the University of Paris. He died only two years later, also of leukemia.

Marguérite Perey, an accomplished student of physics, began working in Marie's lab in 1929, when she was only twenty years old. Ten years later she discovered an entirely new radioactive element, francium, which (in Marie's own tradition) she named after her native country. Francium, the eighty-seventh element in the periodic table, is the heaviest chemical element of the alkali metal group.

Perey was appointed professor of nuclear chemistry at Strasbourg University, and she served as director of its Nuclear Research Center from 1958 until her death in 1975. She, too, died of cancer believed to be the result of radiation exposure. Perey was the first woman to break the sex barrier of the French Academy of Science, being appointed a member in 1962—an honor refused to her mentor, Marie Curie.

Lise Meitner

NUCLEAR FISSION

The atomic bomb was made possible by a pacifist Jew working in Berlin in the 1930s. Had she known to what uses her discovery of nuclear fission (it was she who coined the term) would be put, Dr. Lise Meitner might never have begun her research. As it was, she retired from the field of atomic physics as soon as the city of Hiroshima was destroyed. "It was an unfortunate accident that this discovery came about in time of war," Meitner said. "I myself have not worked on smashing the atom with the idea of producing death-dealing weapons. Women have a great responsibility, and they are obliged to try so far as they can to prevent another war."

Lise Meitner was born in 1878 in Vienna, to a large Jewish family—although she and her seven siblings were baptized and raised as Protestants, probably to protect them from rampant anti-Semitism. As a youngster, Lise was fascinated by the work of Marie Curie, and entered the University of Vienna in 1901 determined to study the new science of physics, even though such work by a female was discouraged and laughed at. When she received her doctorate from that institution in 1906, she became one of the first women to do so.

Dr. Meitner remained in Vienna for some time after her graduation, studying the burgeoning field of radioactivity. But it was in Berlin that the greatest advances were being made in the study of the atom, and it was there that she relocated in 1908. She studied under Dr. Max Planck, who would win the Nobel Prize for his theory of quantum mechanics. Lise was Planck's assistant for three of his most productive years.

While she worked with Dr. Planck Lise met Dr. Otto Hahn, who would become her lifelong collaborator. Since Emil Fischer would allow no women in his Chemical Institute, Meitner and Hahn set up a research lab in a carpenter's workshop, which they equipped to measure radiation and conduct experiments in the formation of new elements.

The First World War created a break in Dr. Meitner's work: She enlisted in the Austrian Army as a nurse and radiographer. During her leaves, she continued to work with Hahn on the measurement of radioactive substances. In the last months of the war, their studies led to the creation of a new element, which they named protactinium.

The status of women changed abruptly during World War I, since those who took up positions of responsibility by necessity proved they also could compete by choice. In 1918 Dr. Meitner was appointed head of the physics department at the prestigious Kaiser Wilhelm Institute and was asked to organize a division to study radioactivity. In 1926 she became a full professor of physics at the University of Berlin, where she continued to study the correlation between gamma and beta rays.

Dr. Meitner's groundbreaking discovery was made after she began working once again with Dr. Hahn, in 1934. Intrigued by the work of Enrico Fermi, who had been bombarding heavy elements (like uranium) with neutrons and creating new elements even heavier than the one he started with, Lise and Otto set out to repeat his experiments. It was Lise who noticed the cataclysmic discrepancy that would unlock atomic energy.

While bombarding uranium with slow-speed neutrons, the scientists were amazed to detect the presence of barium in the final product, a lighter-than-uranium element that had no evident reason to be there. Lise Meitner and Otto Hahn had just split the atom, although neither of them realized it at the time.

Just as Lise's experiment were coming to a head, so was the power of the Nazi Party. Even though she was never a practicing Jew, neither did she keep her birthright a secret. She was summarily dismissed from her position at the University of Berlin, and—now that the Nazis had absorbed Austria—her foreign citizenship was no protection. She had to flee for her life.

Only Dr. Hahn knew that Lise's "vacation" in Holland was a cover for a prearranged exodus to Sweden. Lise got to Holland with the help of friends, and she slipped across the North Sea to Denmark barely ahead of Nazi patrol boats. In Copenhagen she stayed with physicist Niels Bohr and his wife.

Safely in Stockholm, working at the new Nobel Institute for Physics, Meitner published an earthshaking paper. She and her nephew Otto Frisch were duplicating some of Otto Hahn's experiments when Lise realized the significance of splitting the nucleus of a uranium atom. She calculated the potential release of energy in such an event, using Einstein's equation $E = mc^2$, and told the world that the nucleus of a uranium atom could release twenty million times more energy than exploding an equal amount of TNT. The nuclear age began—for better or worse—when Dr. Meitner published her findings in the British journal *Nature* on January 16, 1939.

German-Jewish physicist Lise Meitner (shown here in 1949) was fleeing the Nazis when her theory of atomic fission was co-opted for weapon research. The true mother of the A-bomb never claimed—nor desired—the title. UPI/BETTMANN NEWSPHOTOS

Immediately after the publication of Dr. Meitner's study, the world powers raced to convert this source of energy into a destructive weapon. Dr. Meitner had no interest in turning her "promised land of atomic energy" into a bomb. Invited to work on the Manhattan Project, she refused and said that she hoped the weapon project would fail. Two days after the bomb was dropped on Hiroshima, Dr. Meitner had a conversation with First Lady Eleanor Roosevelt. "I hope," said Dr. Meitner, "that it will be possible to . . . prevent such horrible things as we have had to go through." Dr. Meitner said she was surprised that her theoretical work had been turned into such a vicious force with such rapidity.

In 1945 Dr. Meitner was elected to the Swedish Academy of Science, the third woman in history to receive that honor. In 1946 she came to the United States and was a visiting professor at Catholic University in Washington, D.C., for a year. In 1947, at age sixty-nine, she retired from the Nobel Institute and worked in a small lab at the Royal Academy for Engineering Sciences, where she designed a nuclear reactor for the Swedish Atomic Energy Commission.

In 1958 Lise moved to England to join her family; her nephew Otto Frisch—now Dr. Otto Frisch—was chairman of the natural philosophy department at Cambridge University, and that is where she settled. She continued to lecture and travel, but by 1966 she was too frail to go to Vienna to accept the $50,000 Enrico Fermi Award voted her for her achievements. She was the first woman to receive that ironic honor, which she shared with Dr. Hahn and Dr. Fritz Strassman, another colleague. The chairman of the U.S. Atomic Energy Commission, Dr. Glenn Seaborg, traveled to Cambridge to present her with her award personally.

Lise Meitner was a soft-spoken woman with a strong Austrian accent. She loved music and is said to have had "an easy smile." She died in a nursing home in England on October 27, 1968, only a few days before her ninetieth birthday. Dr. Otto Hahn, her coworker of thirty years, had died three months earlier. She never accepted or approved of the uses to which her discovery was put, and she never received the Nobel Prize for her breakthrough, an honor that Hahn received in 1944.

Chien-Shiung Wu

ATOMIC PARITY

One of the most honored scientists of our day is Dr. Chien-Shiung Wu, a native of China who immigrated to the United States to attend college. Dr. Wu holds honorary degrees from Princeton, Smith, Rutgers, and Yale; was the first woman to receive the Comstock Prize for the National Academy of Sciences and the Research Corporation Award; and was the seventh woman in history appointed to the National Academy of Sciences. In 1976 President Gerald Ford handed her the U.S. National Medal of Science. (Most of her financial honors are bequeathed to scholarships for Chinese youngsters.)

Dr. Wu is best known for experimentally disproving a long-held theory of physics called "the conservation of parity" in 1956. Technically speaking, Dr. Wu proved the existence of "parity violation," a discovery that shook the very foundations of physics. Like Einstein's Theory of Relativity, the concept of parity violation changed the way scientists looked at the structure of the universe.

Dr. Wu's colleagues in the study, Dr. Tsung-Dao Lee and Dr. Chen-Ning Yang, were awarded the Nobel Prize in 1957 for their theoretical contributions to the project. Dr. Wu, who did the actual experimental proof, was overlooked.

The law of parity states that like atomic particles always act alike; that nature is totally symmetrical, and an atomic system is identical in nature to its own mirror image. Dr. Wu's experiment

153

with the emission of electrons at ultralow temperatures proved that atomic particles do not behave symmetrically; that there is "right-handedness" and "left-handedness," and different systems obey distinct patterns. The long-standing assumption of atomic parity was disproved, and a door was opened for innumerable leaps in theoretical physics.

"I wonder whether the tiny atoms and nuclei, or the mathematical symbols or the DNA molecules, have any preference for either masculine or feminine treatment," said Dr. Wu in 1965, pointing out the irrationality of another long-held scientific assumption: that men are more suited to the field than women.

Born in 1912 near Shanghai, Wu was encouraged to study science by her father, a school principal, and her two brothers. She received her bachelor's degree at National Central University in Nanking in 1934, and she continued her studies in 1936 at the University of California at Berkeley. There she met physics student Chi-Liu ("Luke") Yuan; they married in 1942 and had a son in 1945.

After receiving her doctorate in physics, Dr. Wu (she never used her married name professionally) was asked to work for the Manhattan Project at Columbia University in New York, where she developed a process for producing large quantities of fissionable uranium and perfected an improved Geiger counter. Coworkers remarked on how soft-spoken and feminine she was, and made gentle sport of her preference for the traditional Chinese mode of dress.

After the war, then-Assistant Professor of Physics Wu was approached by scientists Lee and Yang to help them with their theoretical analysis of atomic parity. It was a long and complex experiment, but it finally blew holes in a theory of atomic physics that had stood for three decades.

Today Dr. Wu is a full professor at Columbia, remaining vital and active into her seventies. Her current work involves using advanced biophysics to find a cure for sickle-cell anemia.

Maria Goeppert-Mayer / Marguerite Chang / M. Hildred Blewett / Leona Libby

THE ATOMIC BOMB

There are, surprisingly, quite a few women scientists involved in development of the weapons that Lise Meitner's discovery of nuclear fission made possible. Dr. Maria Goeppert-Mayer was part of the team that first isolated fissionable uranium-235, and she was present when the first atomic pile was constructed. Dr. Leona Libby was an appointed member of World War II's Manhattan Project—the group of scientists who built the atomic bomb. M. Hildred Blewett designed today's state-of-the-art particle accelerator, enabling scientists to free even more energy from the nucleus of the atom. Dr. Marguerite Chang designed the trigger mechanism for underground nuclear testing.

All these women contributed to both the practical and the theoretical sides of nuclear physics and advanced weaponry, fields of study generally supposed to be entirely male preserves.

Maria Goeppert-Mayer, winner of the Nobel Prize in 1963 for her theoretical analysis of atomic structure—the "shell theory," as it's called—emigrated from her native Poland to Germany, where she took a doctorate in mathematics. Fleeing the Nazis in 1930, Maria Goeppert and her scientist husband, Joseph Mayer, came to the United States; she joined the isotope research team at Columbia University, and he worked "bombsite," at the Aberdeen Proving Grounds in Maryland.

Their work, individually and combined, was instrumental in the perfection of the atomic bomb, although Maria is remembered more for her work in theoretical mathematics than for hardware inventions. The Drs. Goeppert-Mayer ended their careers as professors at the University of California at San Diego; semiparalyzed by a stroke in 1960, Maria continued to teach and study for more than a decade until her death in 1972 at age sixty-five.

Dr. Leona Marshall Libby was told by one coworker to "go back to pots and pans" when she was chosen as the only woman officially assigned to the Manhattan Project. "She just outworked and outshone the best of them," recalled her son, John Marshall III, on the occasion of her death in 1986.

As an inventor, Dr. Libby not only helped design and build the first nuclear reactor, she also personally directed the construction of the first thermal column and invented the advanced analytical machine called a "rotating neutron spectrometer." In a tangential area, Dr. Libby discovered the method through which historical climates are measured from isotope residue in the rings of trees.

Dr. Libby never regretted being instrumental in designing the atomic bomb, saying that its use at the end of World War II saved more lives than it took. She ended her days as a professor at the University of California at Los Angeles, dying at age sixty-seven from what is assumed to be a radiation-induced illness.

M. Hildred Blewett is a physicist of the nuts-and-bolts variety, one of the rare "mechanics" who can create the equipment needed to prove the most rarefied of scientific theories. Her inventions include advancements to the proton synchrotron and other arcane pieces of technology that magnetize and accelerate atomic particles no eye can see. A Canadian by birth, Blewett now travels the world advising on the design of state-of-the-art nuclear accelerators, including the CERN in Switzerland and the Saturne in France.

Dr. Marguerite Shue-Wen Chang, a graduate of Louisiana's Tulane University by way of Nanking, China, invented the device that triggers underground nuclear test explosives. A research chemist for the U.S. Department of the Navy, Dr. Chang's achievements are mostly classified information, but it is known that she has significantly advanced the study of missile propellants and advanced explosives. Her work has earned her two special awards from the Navy, and the Federal Women's Award (1973) for outstanding government service. She continues to work closely with the Atomic Energy Commission and is particularly concerned with personnel safety and quality control in the field of weapons manufacture.

Nuts and Bolts

OF ALL THE scientific disciplines, engineering is most completely a male preserve. In a 1981 encyclopedic book called *Great Engineers and Pioneers of Technology,* not one woman was included. While even today women make up only 3 percent of working engineers, their contributions have been significant far beyond their actual numbers.

Since 1952 the Society of Women Engineers has been recognizing meritorious achievement in everything from waste management to solid state electronics. Women excel in weaponry, metallurgy, computer engineering, and architectural design.

Female engineers include the likes of Sirvart A. Mellian, a research and development designer with the U.S. Army who specializes in ballistics. Her Patent No. 4,183,097 covers the invention of contoured protective body armor used by law-enforcement personnel in most major metropolitan areas. Another military researcher and inventor is Jenny Bramley, who holds nineteen patents in night optics. And Marguerite M. Rogers designs sophisticated air-delivered tactical weapons for the Navy.

Few think of women in connection with fluid mechanics, yet Sheila Widnall designed M.I.T.'s advanced wind tunnel facility; Christine Darden serves a similar function for NASA. Barbara Crawford Johnson also is affiliated with NASA and is the person who decided the reentry pattern for the *Apollo-Soyuz* space mission.

Hertha Ayrton, who in 1898 became the first woman elected to Britain's Institution of Electrical Engineers, invented a sphygmograph (a machine for monitoring the human pulse), but her specialty was studying the behavior of the electrical arc. During World War I, she standardized the various types of searchlights for the British military, and she invented the Ayrton Fan for dispersing mustard gas.

Laurence Delise Pellier pioneered stainless steel and titanium alloys in the 1950s. Esther Conwell was instrumental in the development of semiconductors. Aerospace engineer Marjorie Rhodes Townsend patented a digital telemetry system. Chemical engineer Elizabeth Drake invented a fractionation apparatus.

Laurence Cantenot, a Frenchwoman still in her thirties and reportedly a great beauty, has designed a new retrieval system for silos, even though her specialty is aeronautical engineering. Her "masterpiece of simplicity" costs ten times less than its predecessors and works ten times as fast.

So much for *Great Engineers*.

Eleanor Raymond / Maria Telkes / Stella Andrassy

THE SUN-WORSHIPERS

Solar energy is unquestionably the perfect power source: It's completely nonpolluting, it's absolutely free, and there's not a chance under the sun of running out of it. But it took three pioneering women—an architect, an engineer, and a Hungarian countess—to prove it could be used for something more productive than a flattering tan.

Architect Eleanor Raymond invented the first solar-heated house in collaboration with chemist-*cum*-engineer Maria Telkes. Located in Dover, Massachusetts, the house was built in 1948 as an experiment and still is used. "I acted as the catalyst," recalls Raymond. "Miss Amelia Peabody [the property owner] had the money and the interest in experimentation, and Dr. Telkes had the theories."

The Dover solar house was the first to use passive solar design, which depends on nothing but sunshine itself for heat, rather than "active solar" photovoltaic panels, which generate electricity. Despite theoretical clues about how the sun would interact with the house environment, in the final analysis it was up to the architect and her blueprints to make it work. And heating a house throughout the Massachusetts winter was no mean feat.

"When the door opened to me on Christmas Eve [1948] and I was greeted with a flood of warm air that I knew had to have come only from the sun—that was thrilling!" says Raymond with a smile.

Raymond, who was singled out for the Institute of Architects' highest honor, also designed the first "modern" house in Massachusetts following a trip to Europe, where she was exposed to the Bauhaus movement. She was famous for her innovative use of nontraditional material, building an all-plywood house in 1940 and an all-Masonite house in 1944.

She was also noted for the environmentally sensitive residential buildings she constructed throughout New England. "I design houses from the inside out, for I like to establish a connection between the inside and the outdoors," she said. "I love balconies and decks that you can walk out on and enjoy. Then, if the inside rooms are small, you don't feel closed in—there's a richness of relationship between inside and out."

Maria Telkes, Raymond's partner in the Dover solar house, was born in Hungary, and immigrated to the United States in 1927. She has invented and patented numerous solar-powered devices, including a still for life rafts, a solar oven, and heating equipment for houses. Her distinguished career has included research positions at Westinghouse, M.I.T., and New York University's College of Engineering, and she is the former research director of solar engineering at the Princeton Division of Curtiss-Wright Corporation and for the Institute for Direct Energy Conversion of the University of Pennsylvania.

Besides Raymond, Telkes collaborated with another early solar advocate—Countess Stella Andrassy. Born in Sweden to a titled family, Countess Andrassy followed in her mother's footsteps and studied to become a concert pianist, although in college she took many science courses as well. She married Count Irme Andrassy of Hungary, an electrical engineer-*cum*-diplomat, in 1919. They lived a comfortable life in the waning days of the European nobility until the onslaught of World War II.

In an escape reminiscent of the Von Trapps' in *The Sound of Music,* the countess and her husband fled with their three children, one grandchild, their pet dogs, and several horses across the Alps when the Russians invaded in 1945. This is the first time she remembers being "inventive." "We spent eight weeks between the Russian and German lines, being shot at by all sides. You had to be inventive in those circumstances just to survive," she recalled in a recent interview.

When they arrived in New York, the Andrassys met their fellow Hungarian émigré, and the countess began assisting Dr. Telkes to help support her newly impoverished family. The countess has patented nine solar-powered inventions in all, including a food drier, an oven, a water heater, and a still for turning seawater into fresh water. Her last patent was filed five years ago in Canada, for a method to extract oil from Canada's huge tar sand fields. "It's a hot-water method, but something else was needed," she explained. "Then I remembered that mixing mayonnaise with oil extracts the egg, so I tried mixing some of the oil with the hot water and tar sand. It worked. Clear oil rose to the top of the containers, where it could be siphoned off."

America hasn't exactly embraced solar power, but Andrassy is not bitter. "In this country, where everything is push-button, it can be expected that people would be slow to accept solar energy. But the Third World can't afford to wait, which is why they've expressed the most interest in my solar inventions." She says that her solar food drier has been especially popular with people in less developed countries, since much of their diet consists of dried fruits and vegetables. "The solar drier accelerates the drying process and keeps the food sanitary and pest-free. Just this year I dried some grapes into raisins, which previously it was said could not be done."

Now eighty-four years old, the countess still is inventing. She lives close to Princeton University in New Jersey and continues to use their research facilities. Her latest invention, which she has yet to patent, is a method for turning sewer sludge into sterilized fertilizer—with distilled water as the by-product! A 330-square-foot experimental prototype has been built at Princeton.

Kate Gleason

THE TRACT HOUSE

For better or for worse, mass-produced, low-cost tract housing was the invention of a woman, Kate Gleason, who conceived of the first "development" at East Rochester, New York, at the end of the First World War. By 1921 Kate was selling $4,000 concrete boxes (she also invented the method for pouring the concrete) to young families for a down payment plus $40 a month, and she set a precedent for every suburb in America.

Born in 1865, Kate Gleason was a tomboy and an avid competitor. "If we were jumping from the shed roof, I chose the highest spot," she recalled. "If we vaulted fences, I picked the tallest." She earned pocket money as a teenager working in her father's machine shop, and later she was forced to drop out of Cornell University to help him run the operation.

Kate became the traveling salesperson representing the Gleason Works and reportedly was a big hit in the male-dominated world she broached. In 1893 she helped her father perfect a machine that produced beveled gears faster and cheaper than earlier devices could, and the family firm made a good living selling the gears to the fledgling auto industry. Oddly enough, Kate rather than her father was credited with the invention, one of the rare cases where a woman has been mistakenly remembered for a man's idea, not the other way around. Henry Ford himself once referred to the Gleason gear planer as "the most remarkable machine work ever done by a woman."

In 1913 Kate Gleason saw a crying need for affordable housing in her community and decided to find a way to utilize automotive mass-production methods in housing construction. In a time when all houses were custom-built—as clothing was custom-made before the advent of ready-to-wear—she built a one-hundred-house development called Concrest, where each six-room home would provide small luxuries like a gas range, built-in bookcases, mirrors, and ironing boards—yet still remain affordable for working-class families. "My particular inspiration for [mass-production] methods came," she once wrote, "from a visit I made to the Cadillac factory, when Mr. Leland showed me the assembly of the eight-cylinder engine."

To make the ticky-tacky houses of Concrest appear individualized, Miss Gleason would orient each home differently on its plot, a ploy still used today. She employed similar methods at Beaufort, South Carolina, where she built a low-cost recreation colony for artists and writers. In 1927 she built a concrete community in Sausalito, California, based on the principles of Indian adobe construction.

Kate Gleason died in 1933 at age sixty-eight, a wealthy and respected general contractor.

Harriet Irwin

THE HEXAGONAL HOUSE

In 1888 the Western New York Association of Architects held its annual convention, during which the organization's president, Sidney Smith, prefaced his address with this greeting: "Gentlemen: I wish I could add 'ladies,' but I hope the day is not very distant when I can." Mr. Smith was misinformed; in 1888 a housewife from North Carolina had been a working architect for nearly twenty years.

Harriet Morrison Irwin was the first woman in the United States to patent an architectural innovation. On August 24, 1869—with no formal training to call upon—Mrs. Irwin submitted to the U.S. Patent Office a plan for "a hexagonal building." From these plans she built her home—which stands to this day.

In many respects, Harriet Irwin was the epitome of the antebellum, bluestocking southern belle. Her father was the first president of Davidson College; her brother-in-law was famed Confederate hero Stonewall Jackson. Having grown up in Charlotte, North Carolina, in the golden era of Dixie, Mrs. Irwin watched much of the Reconstruction from her bed: She had given birth by that time to nine children, five of whom survived infancy. The business of running a household proved to be a demanding one.

If her work environment was to be her home, at least she could improve that environment to make her work easier, she decided. She recognized the need to replace the Greco-Roman palaces of yesteryear, but she took issue with the Victorian boxes that were offered in their place. Irwin felt that homes designed by men for men were ill suited for the business of running them.

One architectural critic of the day threw the gauntlet at women's feet when he wrote: "Women are eternally complaining of closet room, of badly arranged rooms and closets, of the want of windows for ventilation, of the inaccessibility of some of the most important sections; attics, for example, and various other shortcomings, found in some of the most costly as well as the poorest houses, yet they have not seemed to think of the remedy in providing better designs and calling public attention to them."

Harriet picked up the gauntlet—but what did a middle-aged southern belle know about designing a house? Admittedly, next to nothing, but she found out. Poring over architectural volumes such as *The Theory of Strains in Girders* and Mrs. Tuthill's *History of Architecture* (the first architectural history written by a woman),

Harriet learned the difference between a flying buttress and a riser.

Her goal was to build nothing less than a "cheaper, handsomer" dwelling "capable of greater artistic beauty than the square." In short, she proposed "an entire revolution in the method of building houses." Irwin's concepts were highly advanced for their gingerbread-castle day.

"The objects of my invention," she said, "are the economizing of space and building materials, the obtaining of economical heating mediums, through lighting and ventilation, and facilities for inexpensive ornamentation."

Utilizing a hexagonal design, she increased floor space and improved "every facility of communication between the different rooms." No longer would the woman be stuck most of her working day in a dark kitchen at the end of a long hallway in the back of the house. Each room would now be interconnected in a continuous circular pattern. This synthesis of form and function, of biology and technology, would later be known as ergonomics.

In addition to the hexagonal house—an elegant, two-story structure with a mansard roof and central tower, which still stands on Charlotte's West Fifth Street—Harriet built two other dwellings along more conventional lines.

Harriet Irwin had a second career as a writer, authoring the mystical/philosophical novel *The Hermit of Petraea* (in which the hero discovers an Arabian hexagonal house, among other things), numerous magazine and newspaper articles, and the beginning of a book on the history of colonial Charlotte. She died in 1897, reportedly a "gentle, sweet, lovable old lady." Inventive to the very end, she designed her own hexagonal tombstone.

Martine Kempf

VOICE-CONTROLLED WHEELCHAIR

Martine Kempf was a twenty-three-year-old astronomy student in 1982 when she first designed a computer program that would respond to spoken commands. By the time she was twenty-seven, the Katalavox (from the Greek *katal,* to understand, and the Latin *vox,* meaning voice) was being used to operate voice-activated microscopes and wheelchairs, and Martine had set up shop in California's Silicon Valley to manufacture and market the sophisticated invention.

Raised in the Alsace-Lorraine region of France, Martine attended university at Bonn, Germany. Her invention was inspired by her father, a polio victim, who designed a hand-controlled automobile for his own use and later made a business of customizing cars for the handicapped. Martine began to work on the voice-activator when she saw armless German teenagers—Thalidomide victims—who had no way to maneuver their wheelchairs. A wheelchair that responded to voice commands seemed the solution.

Her Katalavox is twenty times more efficient than comparable models that established computer firms had been perfecting for years—and she created it on a home Apple P.C. Although the Katalavox is being used for wheelchairs, its main application is in microsurgery, allowing doctors hands-free manipulation of magnifying equipment. The little black box—smaller than a clock radio and weighing less than five pounds—also is being tested for use on the Space Shuttle and in automobiles.

167

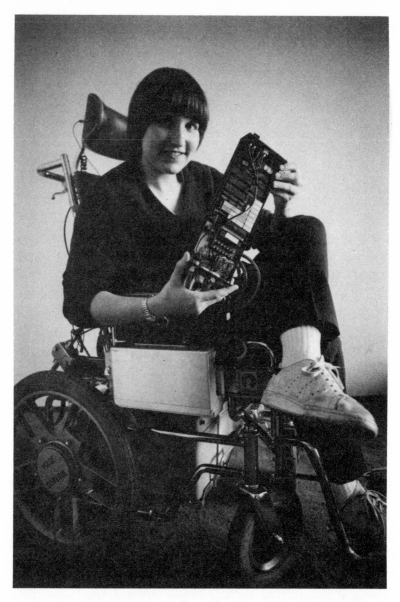

Martine Kempf was only twenty-three when she perfected the Katalavox, a piece of computer magic that allows the handicapped to give verbal orders to wheelchairs and doctors to operate delicate equipment by voice comand. KATY RADDATZ/ *People Weekly*/© 1986 Time Inc

Kempf received the Prix Grand Siècle Laurent Perrier for her contribution to microsurgery, and she expects to capture 10 percent of the U.S. microsurgery market with her device. Martine—who speaks three languages fluently, pilots her own plane, and plays classical piano, violin, and bassoon—says she hopes to join forces with the Jet Propulsion Laboratory or another American space research facility in the near future. Her dream is to be the first Earthwoman on Mars.

Mildred Mitchell

BIONICS

Scientists were fascinated with the concept of bionics long before the advent of television's popular *Six Million Dollar Man*. Although the term usually is considered a cross between biology and electronics, there are those who say it should be considered simply the Greek term for "lifelike" and that such basic inventions as imitating animals by wearing their skins for warmth can be called a bionic art. But that is not the aspect of bionics that fascinates Mildred Mitchell, who holds advanced degrees in mathematics, philosophy, and psychology.

A member of the Aerospace Medical Research Laboratory since 1958 and more recently head bionicist at the Air Force Avionics Laboratory, Dr. Mitchell first entered bionics through her expertise in psychology. In 1960 she led the isolation studies on the Project Mercury astronauts and served on the panel that evaluated the candidates. Dr. Mitchell specializes in adapting electronics to perform human functions, especially in space. Her artificial mus-

169

cle, composed of 130,000 separate fibers, can lift heavy equipment accurately and efficiently when a human muscle is incapacitated—as, for instance, in the high gravity of a takeoff or landing. A small device Dr. Mitchell calls the "nail bender" can, in fact, bend an iron nail with a puff of air.

Dr. Mitchell's work also has created man-made "biological clocks," duplicating through machinery the natural mechanism that tells animals whether it is day or night, even if their environment has been artificially altered.

A long-range project for Dr. Mitchell's team is creating a means of communicating information through touch, simulating the tactile sensory system using tiny jets of air. Many of these innovations will have as much or more importance as aids to the handicapped on earth than practicality in space.

Harriet W. R. Strong

WATER CONTROL ENGINEER

In 1883 Harriet W. R. Strong reached the low point of her life. Her husband of twenty years, Charles, committed suicide after losing the family fortune in a silver mining scam. What was left of the Strong estate was so encumbered in lawsuits that it would take another eight years before a settlement was reached. A semi-invalid since childhood, Harriet was faced with the seemingly insurmountable task of supporting her four children on what was left—220 acres of semi-arid land in Southern California, near the present-day city of Whittier.

Harriet Strong knew next to nothing about farming and even less about earning a living.

Ten years later, she would be known as the Walnut Queen for her agricultural prowess; become the first woman elected to the Los Angeles Chamber of Commerce; the first president of the new feminist Business League of America; and gain national attention at the World's Columbian Exposition in Chicago for her patented irrigation system.

Born in 1844 in Buffalo, New York, Harriet led a nomadic life as a child and suffered from what was diagnosed as an "affliction of the spine" that made her weak and sickly. She married a man who was a devoted husband and loving father to their four daughters—but prone to nervous breakdowns, which continued throughout the twenty years of their marriage.

After her husband's premature death in 1883, Harriet analyzed her rather desperate situation and realized that if she were to be the breadwinner in the family, she would simply have to get healthy. Following a visit to a Philadelphia neurologist, she pronounced herself cured, and—according to people who knew her then—more than just her physical condition changed. Where there had been a sweet and obedient wife was now an independent woman full of vitality and resolve.

Mrs. Strong researched which crops were performing well in the arid Southern California climate and chose a relative newcomer, walnuts, as her first crop. Eventually her orchard became the largest in the world—some twenty-five miles long—and she was the first to introduce winter irrigation of the crop. This she followed with citrus fruits, pomegranates, and pampas grass (used for decorative purposes).

When a lack of water threatened to ruin her first harvest, she designed and patented a flood control/storage dam system. (She also successfully patented several household inventions.) The irrigation system was unique in that the design incorporated a succession of dams that ensured safety in case of a break, utilized the pressure of the water itself for structural support of the preceding dam, and regulated water flow in a controlled, uniform manner. The system was adopted by engineers as far away as Central America, and received an award from the federal Agricultural and Mining departments.

During World War I, Congress considered using it as a model for the first development of the Grand Canyon and Colorado River as a source of irrigation water and generation of electricity. The development of the region was considered vital to the war effort and twice she was called before Congress for expert testimony.

The cessation of the war in 1918 temporarily suspended the Grand Canyon project. However, her early advocacy, including the introduction of two bills in Congress, was an important step in the eventual development of the Colorado River, which in turn provided the water necessary for the rapid growth of Southern California as one of the world's great urban and food-producing regions.

The Naturalists

CHANGING THE ENVIRONMENT is the oldest calling of invention; and it probably was a woman who first cultivated a crop or built a hut. The shapers and growers have become more sophisticated as society's needs have changed. Today the hutmakers are architects and solar engineers, the crop-tenders are botanists and entomologists. Those who seek to improve the world around us have done so for motives ranging from pure intellectual curiosity, like biochemist Wanda K. Farr, to commercial gain, like vintner Nicole-Barbe Clicquot. Regardless of the motivation, the results have affected our landscape.

Some innovators in the environmental sciences have not been included here because they did not devise or patent concrete items. Any study of the world around us should not overlook the vital contributions of Ellen Richards (1842–1911), the mother of ecology

173

and the first to teach, at M.I.T., about the interrelationships of water, air, and our food system. (Her standard-bearer, Ruth Patrick, does earn a mention because, among other accomplishments, she patented a pollution-detection device called the diatometer.)

Other women who made significant contributions in this field are Russian-born Katherine Esau, who conducted important research in the structure of plant tissue and the transmittal of plant diseases; botanist Kate Furbish, who in her ninety-seven years compiled sixteen folio volumes of illustrations and four thousand sheets of dried plants; German botanical and entomological illustrator Maria Sibylla Merian (1647–1717), who by keeping live insect specimens was the first to trace their development at each stage of growth; Dora Hayes, who as chief of the Chemical and Biophysical Laboratory at the Beltsville (Maryland) Agricultural Research Center was the first to send insects into space; U.S. Department of Agriculture chemist Odette Shotwell, who has developed a cancer-producing toxin from molds; biologist Lucille Farrier Stickel, who published numerous papers on pesticide residue in wildlife; and Helen B. Correl, specialist in aquatic and wetlands plants.

Since the U.S. Patent Office began to register plant hybrids, many hobby gardeners—male and female—have become patent-holders by growing white roses, yellow cucumbers, and square watermelons. For the sake of space, these inventors will have to wait for another book to see their creations lauded.

Eleanor A. Ormerod

INSECT CONTROL

When she died in 1901, Eleanor A. Ormerod was the most honored British woman scientist of her day and one of the most celebrated of any nationality or either sex. She had received every conceivable award in the field of entomology; been appointed to scientific societies in England, the United States, Russia, Canada, and Australia; and served as consulting entomologist to the Royal Agricultural Society. Her greatest accomplishment, though, was bringing the study of insects out of the academic halls and into the fields.

Ormerod invented efficient, inexpensive methods for the eradication of injurious insects, and for the first time in history brought a systematic approach to saving crops and livestock from their ravages. Her pamphlets and annual reports on pest control, which she produced at her own expense, were the first published guides for farmers on the subject.

Ormerod was an unlikely candidate for a scientific career. Born in 1828 to the English upper class (her grandfather had served as physician to the king), she should have married in her late teens or early twenties and retired to the comfortable, if not entirely fulfilling, life of a squire's wife. However, Eleanor was also seemingly born with the scientist's inclination to question the accepted—especially where it concerned her own abilities.

And she delighted in doing the unexpected. A friend recalled a scene at a luncheon party: "The peace of the entertainment was suddenly disturbed by the arrival of a large and lively hornet. No one else ventured to interfere with the enemy, but Miss Ormerod waited quietly till the insect came close to her, caught it in one of the little chip boxes which she generally carried in her pockets. I leave you to imagine the astonishment and admiration of the other guests." Eleanor would later disclose to her confidante that she knew it was a harmless drone by the length of the antennae.

Ormerod never married, instead devoting her life to her chosen field. She worked anonymously for decades, then in 1877 began to publish her *Annual Report of Observations of Injurious Insects*. The pamphlets immediately became popular, requiring print runs as high as 170,000. Soon agriculturalists throughout the world were corresponding with her, and for the next twenty years she became a clearinghouse for entomological information.

Although her research was meticulous and scholarly—she once constructed her own meteorological observation station because she felt climatic data could be useful in her work—her published reports offered commonsense remedies utilizing easily available ingredients. The cure for the turnip moth, she found, was a boiled saline solution. Her widely published remedy for a maggot plaguing livestock—"a dab of cart grease and sulphur applied to the infested area of the hide"—is credited with saving half the cows and oxen in England in the late 1800s.

Her knowledge of injurious insects was so well respected that government officials from Russia to America frequently consulted with her. When the Mediterranean caterpillar threatened widespread destruction of the stored flour inventory in the United States in 1889, the chief entomologist of the Agricultural Department wrote in desperation to Miss Ormerod for the remedy and promptly received this advice: "Get the managers of the steam-mills to turn on the steam to scald them."

More than strictly an entomologist, she was a genuine ecologist who could see beyond the narrow focus of her own scientific pursuit. When a grower complained of a failed watercress crop in an area otherwise free of infestation, she successfully identified the problem as the landlord's wife's fancy for encouraging herons. "The herons cleared off the insect-loving trout, so the vegetable eating-insects got ahead." She assumed the unpopular task of confronting the various "sparrow clubs" popular in England in the late 1800s, some of which cited biblical references to justify their efforts to preserve and encourage the breed. The house sparrow was not only damaging to orchards but also drove off other birds, such as swallows and martins, that consumed far more insects.

Upon her retirement, the *Times* of London wrote that "she has revolutionized the subject of agricultural entomology, as it was understood twenty-five years ago. . . . Not only in the British Empire, but in all progressive countries, Miss Ormerod's name takes first rank amongst the Economic Entomologists of the day." Eleanor Ormerod died four months later.

Jane Colden

THE GARDENIA

The gardenia is named after famed eighteenth-century Scottish naturalist Alexander Garden, but it was a colonial American woman who discovered it and gave it that name. Jane Colden was the first to identify the flowery bush as a species of a new genus of Old World plants that had been sitting under the noses of the greatest botanists in Europe for centuries.

Born in 1724, Jane grew up in the countryside of what was then the province of New York. Her father, Cadwallader Colden, had studied medicine in Scotland, then immigrated to the New World. His ambition was to become a scientist, but a career in government administration proved to be more lucrative and he served several times as the royal acting governor of New York.

Cadwallader had, it appears, a Svengali-like relationship with his daughter. Determined that she should not be like other women, whom he considered "idle," he imported a library from England for his daughter's education. He decided that Jane would pursue botany (she had no choice in the matter) since, he theorized, the study was suited to women in general. "Their natural curiosity and the pleasure they take in the beauty and variety of dress seems to fit them for it," he said. But although Mr. Colden encouraged Jane's studies, he drew the line at teaching her Latin, the universal scientific language of the day—he did not think women capable of learning it. He introduced her to his circle of scientist friends but would personally answer their correspondence to her.

Miss Colden excelled in spite of these handicaps. By 1757 she had cataloged more than three hundred regional plant specimens, many of which she illustrated. Garden, one of her father's friends, called her work "extremely accurate." Ultimately, though, Jane was treated as more of an oddity than a colleague; one of her fellow scientists questioned her father about the quality of her cheese-making, in light of the fact that she possessed "so much scientific knowledge."

Sometime before her marriage in 1759, Jane wrote the Edinburgh Philosophical Society about her findings. Her discovery was not recognized until 1770, however, when her description of the gardenia genus was published in the society's journal, *Essays and Observations, Physical and Literary*. She died as Mrs. William Farquhar in 1766, shortly after the death of her only child. Though her career was stymied, Jane Colden is recognized today as one of the first women scientists of the New World.

Ruth Patrick

DIATOMETER

Two women marine biologists have been largely responsible for ushering in the modern-day concern with ecology. Rachel Carson's 1960 book *Silent Spring* catalyzed a grass-roots campaign to stop the reckless use of chemical pesticides and herbicides. As a result, legislation was passed banning the use of DDT, which had severely disrupted the ecological chain and slaughtered indigenous wildlife.

The other ecological heroine of our time is Ruth Patrick, whose invention of a small device called the diatometer made it possible for the first time to determine accurately the presence of pollution in fresh water.

Born in 1907, Dr. Patrick specializes in limnology, the scientific study of freshwater ecosystems; in fact, she cofounded the discipline. Through her research in the laboratory and her countless hours of fieldwork, she established that freshwater bodies are a complex environment whose health depends upon the survival of a delicate chain of microscopic organisms.

She is the foremost expert on the diatom, a single-celled alga that is the basic food for many organisms in the freshwater ecosystem. Diatoms abound in all fresh waters where there is sufficient light. The number of microscopic diatoms—as measured by a diatometer—in a lake or river can determine both the presence and nature of pollutants that might otherwise be undetectable. Dr.

Patrick was the first to recognize the diatom's usefulness in pollution control.

Dr. Patrick earned her master's and Ph. D. degrees from the University of Virginia and later was appointed a full professor of natural science at the University of Pennsylvania. She is the first woman to chair the board of the Academy of Natural Sciences and the first female research director at Du Pont.

In 1975 she was awarded the richest scientific prize in the world: the $150,000 John and Alice Tyler Ecology Award, administered by Pepperdine University in Malibu, California.

Elizabeth Lucas Pinckney

INDIGO

By developing indigo as a commercial crop in the Carolina colonies, Elizabeth Lucas Pinckney not only made herself a wealthy woman but also created a viable economy for an entire sector of the nascent country. Cultivating indigo in continental America had been thought impossible since farmers first failed in the attempt seventy years before Pinckney's experiments, due to the plant's sensitivity to soil and weather conditions. The French-controlled islands in the Caribbean had a virtual monopoly on indigo and its important after-product, dark blue dye. In 1744 this headstrong young woman, through persistent trial-and-error planting, made indigo the single largest cash crop in Colonial America.

Elizabeth—better known as Eliza—Lucas was born in about 1722 to a British Army colonel stationed in the West Indies. She was a feisty and curious youngster and never was discouraged in her intellectual pursuits by her father, who gave her the run of his library and his approval when she mastered Plutarch, Virgil, and Milton. Eliza spoke French, played the flute, and tutored not only her three younger siblings but also the family's black slaves.

In 1738 the Lucas family moved to a plantation on the Wappoo Creek in South Carolina; the following year, Colonel Lucas sailed off for military duty on Antigua, leaving Eliza in total control of that six-hundred-acre plantation and another fifteen-hundred-acre property at Garden Hill. Still a teenager, Eliza was responsible for her family, its business, and the well-being of twenty slaves and an assortment of employees. "It requires . . . more business and fatigue than you can imagine," seventeen-year-old Eliza wrote to a friend. Twice Eliza turned down proposals of marriage from older, wealthy men, preferring hard work and her independence.

Young Miss Lucas was a clever estate manager, experimenting with new crops for the plantations (ginger, figs, cotton, alfalfa) and helping neighbors with small legal problems. She set a course of instruction for two slave girls, aiming to make them future "school mistres's for the rest of the Negro children," as she put it.

In the first year of her tenure as estate manager, Eliza began toying with the idea of growing indigo on a commercial basis. It would be an important breakthrough for the colonies, if it could be achieved, because producing the valuable blue dye domestically would improve their balance of payments with Britain and free them from trade with the French, who were at war with Britain at the time. Eliza wrote in her journal in 1739 that she "had greater hopes from the Indigo . . . than any of the rest of the things I had tryd."

The Lucas indigo crops grew successfully, but the manufacture of the dye cakes—a complex and delicate process whereby the blue dye is extracted from the indigo plant, refined, and compressed into soluble chunks—was to be a greater obstacle. Colonel Lucas sent a technician up from Montserrat to help make the product, but the specialist sabotaged the first batch by adding "so large a quantity of Lime water as to spoil the color." It turned out that the chemist, Nicholas Cromwell, was worried that cultivation and manufacture of indigo in the American colonies would harm the economy of his own island. Eliza chucked him out of the household and later hired his brother, Patrick, to assist in indigo-making. By 1744 Eliza was able to export seventeen pounds of indigo dye to Britain, and she gave away the bulk of her crop to other Carolina growers so that indigo could be seeded throughout the area.

When the French later made the exportation of indigo a capital crime, they discovered the barn door was being locked after the horse's departure. Eliza Pinckney had established all the thriving indigo the colonies could want. For more than three decades, South Carolina thrived on the income derived from her blue dye cakes, freeing themselves from both British exports and ties to the French-controlled Caribbean. In 1747 South Carolina exported 135,000 pounds of indigo dye. By 1850 the annual exports were as high as a million pounds a year; only the Revolutionary War loosened this tie of commerce, after which Britain turned to the India colonies for its supply.

An established, wealthy plantation owner at age twenty-one, Eliza Lucas finally agreed to marry Charles Pinckney, a highly respected lawyer from Charleston. The two Pinckney sons, Charles and Thomas, became heroes of the Revolutionary War. Both continued their mother's tradition of experimental agriculture, and Charles was one of the first planters to grow the long-staple cotton that was to become the economic bastion (replacing indigo) of the South.

Eliza Pinckney died of cancer on May 26, 1793; President George Washington, by his own request, was a pallbearer at her funeral. Her diaries remain today one of the best sources of information on daily life in eighteenth-century America.

From Eggbeaters to Eggheads

IF THE COMMONLY HELD image of the woman inventor is a housewife who comes up with a better butter mold, that stereotype is effectively demolished by the long and admirable list of pure scientists whose research has led to major technological advances.

Women who were scientists first and inventors second are found in disciplines from astronomy to zero-gravity research. This is all the more remarkable because the vast majority faced tremendous discrimination at the educational institutions they needed to attend. Even in "progressive" New England, females were banned from so much as a grammar-school education until the 1790s and were not allowed to enroll in public high schools until 1852.

Of course, the prejudice within academia was symptomatic of a wider belief that women simply didn't have enough of the gray matter to fill out a white lab coat. As late as 1921, *The New York Times* dismissed the idea that women would ever perform as well as men in pure science, because men "have the power—a necessary qualification for any real achievement in science—of viewing facts abstractly rather than relationally, without overestimating them because they harmonize with previously accepted theories or justify established tastes and properties, and without hating and rejecting them because they have the opposite tendencies."

Ironically, that *Times* editorial was published just after a visit to New York by Marie Curie—physicist, inventor, and two-time Nobel Laureate.

Grace Murray Hopper

COMPUTER COMPILER

In the office of Rear Admiral Grace Murray Hopper hangs a clock that runs counterclockwise. It's her way of reminding visitors that just because something always has been done a certain way doesn't mean it can't be done another way. And she's had to do a lot of reminding in her eighty-one years.

Rear Admiral Hopper revolutionized computer software when she invented the first computer "compiler" in 1952, which allowed for the first automatic programming. Prior to her invention, computer programmers had to write time-consuming machine instructions for each new software package.

"Nobody believed it could be done," she recalled in a recent interview. "Yet it was so obvious. Why start from scratch with every single program you write? Develop one that would do a lot of the basic work over and over again. Developing a compiler was a logical move; but in matters like this, you don't run against logic—you run against people who can't change their minds."

The rear admiral, until she retired in August 1986, was the oldest person on active duty in the U.S. Navy. She joined the U.S. Naval Reserve in 1943, already having earned a Ph.D. in mathematics/physics from Yale. Commissioned as a lieutenant, she was immediately sent to the Navy's Bureau of Ordnance Computation Project at the height of World War II. She retired from the Naval Reserve in 1966 at age sixty, but one year later she was called back to active duty to coordinate the standardization of all Navy computer operations.

While she previously had to deal with only an immediate chain of command, now she heard, "But we've always done it this way" from the entire Navy bureaucracy. "I'm going to shoot somebody for saying that someday," she quips. "In the computer industry, with changes coming as fast as they do, you just can't afford to have people saying that."

Born in New York City in 1906, Hopper comes from an old Navy family. Her great-grandfather—whom she remembers as a distinguished white-haired gentleman with muttonchop whiskers and a silver-topped walking cane—was Rear Admiral Alexander Wilson Russell, who served in the Civil War. She attended Vassar, graduating in 1928, and then attended Yale for graduate studies. She returned to Vassar to teach, and she was an associate professor when she entered the Naval Reserve.

During her wartime assignment, she learned to program the world's first large-scale digital computer: the Mark I. In fact, she was the third person ever to program it. "That was an impressive beast. She was fifty-one feet long, eight feet high, and five feet deep," says Hopper.

Following the war she became a senior programmer with Remington Rand, where she worked on UNIVAC, the first large-scale commercial computer. She was director of automatic programming at Sperry Corporation when she published her first paper on computer compilers, and she is credited with developing COBOL, the first user-friendly business computer software program. COBOL is still widely used today.

Although she has lately been given the praise she deserves for

Indefatigable Grace Hopper finally retired as a rear admiral in the U.S. Navy in 19̲8̲
at the age of eighty, but her spirit of invention is working still. She is credited wit̲
devising COBOL, the first user-friendly computer language, along with many othe̲
technological breakthroughs.

her pioneering contributions to computer science, such was not always the case. "If you do something once, people will call it an accident. If you do it twice, they call it a coincidence. But do it a third time and you've just proven a natural law!" she was once quoted as saying.

Hopper holds honorary doctorates from thirty universities and has published more than fifty scholarly articles, many of which have influenced the design and programming of the modern-day digital computer. Since she is a member of more than sixty professional organizations, her retirement—her second retirement—won't be the leisurely kind. "I seem to do an awful lot of retiring, but I don't think I will ever be able to really retire," she says. "I've always liked to work with either my head or my hands. I'm not content being a spectator."

Betsy Ancker-Johnson

SOLID-STATE PHYSICS

For all our talk about the computer age, computers still use a plodding, forty-year-old system that retrieves information byte by byte. What if someone invented a device that made them "think" by association rather than serially?

"It's the same way the human brain works, by grouping memory in chains of similar information. For example, when you go to the grocery store to find Pepsodent toothpaste, you don't go down every aisle and check every item on the shelves. You naturally go to the area that sells toothpaste," says Dr. Betsy Ancker-Johnson. The computer element she designed to perform this logic task is only one of fifty devices and techniques—mainly in the field of solid-state physics—that she's invented.

Her computer element could revolutionize the industry, but it has yet to be applied because of two problems: It requires a very low temperature within which to function, and it uses an inordinate amount of energy. "Unfortunately, I was called to Washington just after I invented the computer element and have not had time since to work on it. I think that if I had been able to stick around, I would have solved those two problems."

The first project that took Dr. Ancker-Johnson's attention away from her computer element was a stint as assistant secretary of commerce for science and technology—the first female appointee to the position. She managed six divisions with an annual budget of $230 million.

Lately she's being kept busy at General Motors. As vice-president of environmental activities, she heads a staff of two hundred that is responsible for automobile safety, fuel economy, and noise and auto emissions, as well as all waste from GM plants worldwide. "Because of the nature of our work, there isn't a GM product that goes out of the factory that doesn't in some way involve our department," she says.

The discrimination Betsy encountered at graduate school was good training for what she was about to find in the job market. Despite her impeccable credentials, potential employers refused to offer her a job in research because she'd soon quit work to get married. Shut out from industry, she accepted a position as a lecturer at the University of California. "I kept wondering why I had knocked myself out getting that Ph.D. in physics," she recalled.

Although she would keep the job only two years and return to physics research in industry, it was at the University of California that she met her husband, Hal Johnson, a mathematics professor. When he accepted a faculty position at Princeton University, Betsy, who decided to keep her surname, began the job hunt all over again. This time, however, she calmly told her prospective employer, Boeing Aircraft, that, yes, she planned to have children but that all arrangements had already been made for their care: She would import a *Haustochter,* a German nanny, anxious for the opportunity to live in the United States. Impressed by her fore-thought, the interviewer for the research lab hired her on the spot.

Over the next ten years, the Ancker-Johnsons would have two children of their own and adopt two Korean War orphans. Reflecting back on those years as a full-time scientist and mother of four, she admits, "I couldn't have done it without the *Haustochter*. Unfortunately, they have since stopped giving these girls work permits, and I don't know how someone in my shoes could do it today," she says. "Being a woman is still an additional burden. The mother is still the one expected to be responsible for the household and the children."

While working at Boeing, Dr. Ancker-Johnson both designed her computer element and discovered what is today called "the pinch effect" in a semiconductor. "It's a process by which an internal channel within the semiconductor becomes so hot that it melts the path inside," she explains. Her creation of these high temperatures within a crystal was unprecedented and may lead to the development of new materials for computer engineering.

An expert in an esoteric area of physics concerned with plasma in solids, she holds many patents in pure research where there is no immediate application. For example, as a research scientist at Boeing, she led a team of scientists who attempted to extract high-grade aluminum from low-grade ore. The techniques they developed have yet to be employed but have contributed to the store of scientific knowledge of plasma physics.

The first woman at Boeing to have been promoted to middle management, Dr. Ancker-Johnson once conducted an experiment about the company: While working for the Commerce Department, she was helping to revise the patent rights system and tried looking up Boeing's patent assignments. "I never could find out—even as assistant secretary—how many patents Boeing had filed in my name," she says with a laugh.

Although her executive position at GM allows her little freedom to pursue pure research, she hasn't entirely given up the idea of returning to it someday. Her voice still sparkles when recalls the days in the lab. "When I began research, I was looking for new phenomena in physics, and when I came across a new find, it was always very exciting. It seemed that possible applications of these new discoveries would just sort of pop up." In the case of Betsy Ancker-Johnson, what is good for General Motors *is* good for the country.

Mary Engle Pennington

REFRIGERATION, FROZEN FOODS

Few can remember that, earlier in this century, fear of being poisoned from food bought at the local market was an everyday concern. Essential items such as eggs, chickens, fish, and dairy products that had been improperly stored killed hundreds of people every year and made thousands more seriously ill.

America at the turn of the twentieth century was in transition. The urban concentration of previously rural populations combined with the influx of European immigrants meant that tons of food had to be shipped daily into the burgeoning new cities. One of the great challenges of the era was devising a method to move perishables from the farm to the table safely.

More than any other person, Dr. Mary Engle Pennington was responsible for solving this dilemma. Schooled in pure science, she applied her knowledge to the practical. Her design and construction concepts in refrigeration revolutionized the food industry. Her innovations in food transportation and storage as well as her research in frozen foods changed forever the way we eat.

Pennington was born on October 8, 1872, in Nashville, Tennessee, but grew up with her Quaker parents in West Philadelphia. By all accounts, her parents were remarkably progressive for

190

their time. When their daughter decided she would go to the University of Pennsylvania to pursue a degree, the Penningtons barely blanched (although Mrs. Pennington still harbored the hope that one day Mary could be convinced to make a proper debut into Philadelphia society).

Mary completed the Bachelor of Science course requirements in only two years but because she was a woman, the university refused to grant her a degree, instead bestowing upon her a "Certificate of Proficiency." Undaunted by the overt discrimination, she continued postgraduate studies there, where her remarkable performance finally shamed the faculty into granting her a Ph.D. To this day, Pennington remains the only person refused a bachelor's degree but awarded a Ph.D. from a major university.

Employers at the turn of the century were hardly beating down doors to hire professional women. At best, Dr. Pennington was considered an oddity; at worst, an abomination to the natural order of God's universe. So Pennington opened her own business, the Philadelphia Clinical Laboratory, specializing in bacteriological analyses. Her work earned her an appointment as the head of the city health department's bacteriological laboratory, where her research into impure milk established health standards subsequently adopted throughout the country.

Her growing reputation brought her to the attention of Dr. Harvey W. Wiley, chief of the Bureau of Chemistry of the U.S. Department of Agriculture, who fortunately was an old friend of the Pennington family. Wiley needed someone to research the new method of food preservation called refrigeration, and Pennington was the most qualified person to do it. But he also knew bureaucrats would block her appointment as a bacteriological chemist when they found out she was a woman. Under his advice, she signed her 1907 civil service exam "M. E. Pennington." By the time most agricultural officials realized "Mr. Pennington" was a woman, she had already become an indispensable member of the department and first chief of the U.S. Food Research Laboratory.

Pennington didn't actually invent refrigeration, but she made it workable. Like the atmosphere outside, air within a refrigerated locker would lose its ability to hold moisture as it approached freezing temperature. The result was dried-out food; yet, when humidity was increased, the food became moldy. Dr. Pennington solved the problem of humidity control, and her techniques subsequently were adopted by the food, packaging, transportation, and storage industries. Her innovations in refrigeration were so vital during World War I that she was awarded a Notable Service Medal by President Hoover.

Stephanie L. Kwolek

KEVLAR

With almost twenty patents granted for her discoveries, Dr. Stephanie L. Kwolek is one of the most respected research chemists in high-performance textiles. She was given the American Chemical Society Award for creative invention in 1980, for "research in chemistry which contributes to the material prosperity and happiness of people." Her major contribution has been the invention of Kevlar aramid fiber, a thread stronger than steel. It's used in making radial tires, bulletproof vests, boat shells, and in the construction of airplanes and space vehicles. In 1976 she became the first person to spin a polyamide macromolecule from low-temperature liquid crystal solutions.

Stephanie Louise Kwolek was born on July 31, 1923, in New Kensington, Pennsylvania. In 1946 she earned her B.A. in chemistry and took a job with E. I. du Pont de Nemours & Company. "I really wanted to study medicine," says Dr. Kwolek, "but I didn't have enough money to enter medical school. I joined Du Pont as a temporary measure, but the work turned out to be so interesting that I decided to stay on."

Starting as a chemist in the textile fibers department, Kwolek was promoted through the Du Pont ranks. "I think one reason I've stayed here so long," muses Dr. Kwolek, "is that, back in 1946, women were only able to work in the laboratory for a few years, then they'd get pushed into so-called women's jobs. I had something to prove. Also, I was in at the very beginning, when low-temperature polymerization was discovered, and was right there making the discoveries. It was very exciting."

Kwolek first gained national recognition in 1960 for her work creating long molecule chains at low temperatures—synthetic, petroleum-derived fibers that have incredible stiffness and strength. Her discovery of the technology that made spinning these fibers possible led to her winning the American Chemical Society Award for Creative Invention, earned her U.S. Patent No. 3,671,542, and made feasible the commercial production of aramid fibers—a multimillion-dollar industry. Her patents and many scientific honors are awarded to "S. L. Kwolek," a reminder of the time when the wrong gender on a by-line could be a kiss of death.

"The path is easier today," Dr. Kwolek tells the young female scientists whom she teaches and encourages. "There are opportunities for women that did not exist when I started working. Then, if a woman spoke her mind, she quickly found herself out of a job."

Katherine Burr Blodgett

NONREFLECTING GLASS

When General Electric announced the discovery of nonreflecting glass one morning in December 1938, no one was more surprised than Katherine B. Blodgett, the GE research physicist who was responsible for it. After all, she had had the basics of the invention kicking around the lab for the past five years, and no one paid any attention. Suddenly Blodgett found herself being written up in a hundred newspapers across the country.

It's likely that a GE mole warned the company that they'd better make their move quickly or risk losing credit for the invention. Only two days later, physicists from M.I.T. were to present a paper to a science convention detailing their method of making nonreflecting glass.

After receiving a Ph.D. in physics from Cambridge University, Dr. Blodgett went to work at the General Electric lab in Schenectady, New York, where her father had been a patent attorney. She began experimenting with an unusual oily substance developed fifteen years earlier by Dr. Irving Langmuir, who would go on to win a Nobel Prize in chemistry. The substance was unique in that it formed a film on the surface of water—a film exactly one molecule thick. It was an intriguing discovery, but only to physicists; no one could figure out any practical application for it.

One day, while working with the solution, Dr. Blodgett lowered a metal plate into the liquid, and the solution covered the surface. In fact, every time she lowered the plate, another coat would adhere. It was the first time anyone had devised a way of building up layers of molecules one at a time.

She also observed that each layer of molecules reflected light in a slightly different gradation. If there were a device for matching the color with its corresponding layer of thickness, it would then be possible to measure the thickness of film and other extremely thin substances to millionths of an inch. So Blodgett constructed a "color gauge," which consisted of a sealed glass tube containing an inner strip of glass on which successive layers of molecules had been deposited.

When Blodgett applied this gelatinous film to transparent glass, it eliminated all reflection. Clear glass is visible only because of the light it reflects, after all. The light reflected from the film interfered with the light reflected from the glass itself, and the two canceled one another out, rendering the glass invisible.

Blodgett's "invisible glass"—as it was dubbed by the press in 1938—is now used in a variety of optical consumer products, from camera lenses to picture frames. Even more important, her invention made it possible for the first time to measure transparent and semitransparent material in extremely minute degrees. Her invention of an "invisible glass" gauge found use in a variety of disciplines including chemistry, biochemistry, physics, and metallurgy.

This fascinating characteristic aside, the Langmuir-Blodgett film, as it came to be known in the scientific world, had practical applications in optics. Because the film reflected no light, it allowed 100 percent of the light falling on a lens to pass through. Normally, 8 to 10 percent of the light would be lost, reflected from the lens's surface.

Blodgett continued working at GE refining the film until she retired in 1963. For a while, the film was even used successfully in artificial rainmaking, although not in a sufficient degree to make the process practical. She died in 1979 at age eighty-one.

Alice Chatham

SPACE HELMET

When Alice Chatham created one-of-a-kind designs for the stars, she wasn't thinking about Hollywood. As an employee of the Air Force and later NASA, she handmade the helmet worn by Captain Chuck Yeager when he first broke the sound barrier, and she went on to design space helmets for the astronauts.

No one was more surprised than Alice King Chatham, a well-known sculptor in Dayton, Ohio, when the Air Force phoned. It was World War II, and her talents were needed by her country. With the new fighter planes reaching ever-higher altitudes, pilots required a pressurized mask for breathing oxygen to avoid blacking out. And who knew more about the human exterior, reasoned the Air Force scientists, than a sculptor?

After designing and fabricating a leakproof rubber mask for the pilots, Alice was assigned to the top-secret X-1 project. The year was 1947, and the world's first rocket plane was ready to be tested. Her job: Find some way to protect the test pilot from the enormous pressures encountered at an altitude of one hundred thousand feet. What Chatham came up with was, in effect, an artificial environment—a helmet that would fit over the face and ears and be worn with a partial pressure suit.

Successfully testing several prototypes, she went about fashioning the actual helmet worn by the X-1's pilot, Captain Yeager. It consisted of a full-face rubber mask attached to a cloth hood, the mask pressurized by means of an inflatable rubber "bladder" that also covered the ears. A separate hard hat was then placed over the whole thing. It was crude by today's standards, but it did the trick.

Chatham continued to perfect her high-tech headgear, for both supersonic airplanes and early space shots. She created a pressurized suit and full-head helmet with a Fiberglas shell for the "Project Whoosh" chimpanzees, who were ejected from airplanes at speeds faster than sound. She devised a restraining harness and mask for the rhesus monkey that became the first living animal in space. And for "Major," a St. Bernard used to test high-altitude parachutes, she designed a suit to keep the 140-pound "guinea pig" warm.

Along the same lines—but more in keeping with her skills as a sculptor—she designed a test dummy for Project Sierra Sam, which attempted to measure the shock suffered by pilots ejecting from aircraft at high altitude. For the Mercury project she cast the heads of the original seven astronauts and then fitted them with helmets.

Among Chatham's other inventions for NASA are a space bed, stretch-knit garments for astronauts, and various restraints and tethering devices.

Irmgard Flugge-Lotz

AUTOMATIC FLIGHT CONTROL

Ever since man flew his first mechanically powered pair of wings, woman has been right behind him. Besides such well-known flying aces as Amelia Earhart and her British counterpart, Amy Johnson, many women have been instrumental in aeronautical engineering throughout the twentieth century. For example, a Canadian named Elsie Gregory MacGill transformed a railway boxcar plant into an aircraft factory during World War II, producing twenty-three Hawker Hurricane Fighters per week for the Allied effort. And it was Gertrude Rogallo who, assisted by her husband and four children, perfected the hang glider in 1948.

Irmgard Flugge-Lotz was Germany's answer to Elsie MacGill, although Flugge-Lotz was a captive warrior. Her research in shell design and aeronautical engineering led to the development of the first automatic controls in aircraft (a prerequisite to the creation of jet aircraft), but it was conducted under protest.

Born in 1903 in Hameln, Germany, she gravitated toward engineering because of her mother's family's long tradition in the construction trade, combined with her father's career as a mathematician. While other kids went to the local movie theaters to catch the latest by Charlie Chaplin, she attended matinee showings of engineering documentaries. She worked her way through technical university tutoring fellow students in fluid dynamics, and she earned a doctorate in engineering in 1929.

In 1931 she established what became known as the Lotz method for calculating the spanwise (wingtip to wingtip) distribution of a wing's lifting force, which continues to be employed today in aircraft design. She married her colleague Wilhelm Flugge in 1938. Despite their anti-Nazi views, the couple were protected from the Gestapo by Hermann Göring, Hitler's Luftwaffe commander, who overlooked their political heresy to exploit their technical talents. "The balance of power was always precarious." Irmgard's husband would later recall.

Irmgard's specialty was flight dynamics and navigation, and during World War II she began developing her theory of automatic flight control systems. After World War I, the new developments in technology that had dramatically increased the speed of aircraft had not, unfortunately, addressed aircraft control. Pilots still had to control all adjustments manually in ailerons during acceleration and in flying curves; even a slight miscalculation caused the new, faster planes to go into a spin and crash.

Her theory of "discontinuous automatic control" (also the title of her landmark 1953 book) laid the foundation for automatic on-off aircraft control systems, thus making possible the development of jet aircraft.

Lotz and her husband immigrated to the United States after the war. Although Herr Flugge was appointed a professor of engineering at Stanford University, Frau Flugge-Lotz had to settle for becoming a staff lecturer because of the college's antinepotism rules, despite the fact that in 1960, Flugge-Lotz was the only woman delegate to an international conference on automatic flight control. Shortly thereafter she became Stanford's first woman professor of engineering.

Throughout the 1960s she conducted research in satellite control, heat transfer, and the drag characteristics of supersonic aircraft. In 1970 she was appointed a fellow of the American Institute of Aeronautics and Astronautics—the second woman ever so honored—and also received the Achievement Award of the Society of Women Engineers. She died in 1974 at age seventy-one.

Beulah Henry

''LADY EDISON''

In the 1930s, Beulah Louise Henry earned the sobriquet "Lady Edison" for having taken out fifty-two patents in her name. A native of Memphis, Tennessee—who moved to New York City in 1919—Miss Henry was a descendant of colonial hero Patrick Henry on her father's side, and the granddaughter of North Carolina governor William Holden on her mother's. She also suffered from the psychological disorder known as synesthesia, and never quite understood how she made the complex mechanical drawings for her intricate creations. She believed that, due to the odd cross-connections in her brain, she most likely received information from the ether.

Synesthesia, still little understood, was estimated in 1937 to affect 5 percent of the population. It is a dysfunction whereby sound is perceived as color, or taste as touch. Since she was a child, Miss Henry attributed her ability to create mechanical contraptions (while knowing nothing about mechanics) to the same "inner vision" that caused her to see a color and shape for each note of the musical scale.

"I know less than nothing about the laws of physics, mechanics or chemistry," said Beulah in her heyday, having already patented the Protograph (which made four typewritten copies without carbon paper), the bobbinless sewing machine, the "Dolly Dip" sponge (with soap inside), and the "Miss Illusion" doll, whose eyes and hair changed color.

199

The first profitable invention created by Miss Henry—an invention that earned her sufficient royalties to employ a staff of mechanics in her Hotel Victoria laboratory—was an umbrella with snap-on cloth covers (so that the umbrella could instantly match one's wardrobe). Manufacturers all over New York turned her and her umbrella away, saying no snap existed that could adhere fabric to an umbrella rib.

"With a stone for a workbench and a hammer and nails for implements," Miss Henry told *American* magazine in 1925, "I made a hole in the top of that steel rib. Then I got a cake of soap and a nail file, and modeled the style of the snapper that would be strong enough to do duty on a windy day."

The snap-on umbrella was manufactured, was a great success, and was only the first of many ideas that Miss Henry made concrete through sheer inspiration.

Once, the idea for a typewriter silencer—an idea she was to work on for more than ten years—came to Beulah on a street corner. She literally accosted strangers on the sidewalk to borrow a pencil so that she could jot down her concept drawing. Another time, an idea for a children's game occurred to her when she was speaking to a group of people. She stopped in the middle of a sentence, fumbled for a pencil and notepad, leaving her baffled listeners in the lurch as she quickly began sketching the internal mechanism for the invention. Often she would awaken suddenly at three in the morning and begin writing down a new concept.

"My real ambition," Beulah once said, "is to invent or discover something that will exterminate the boll weevil." If she ever did, the discovery was lost to posterity.

FROM UNSUNG
HEROINES TO
CELEBRITY INVENTORS

Unsung Heroines

IN MANY WAYS this entire book is about unsung heroines: women whose contributions to society have, more often than not, escaped its notice. History, like beauty, always has been in the eye of the beholder—or, at any rate, at the mercy of those who record it. And history, at times, has almost malevolently disregarded significant innovations on the part of its distaff side.

In some cases a woman inventor has literally been ripped off for her proceeds. Take Hazel Hook Waltz, who invented the bobby pin in 1916—only to see a large manufacturer patent a minor alteration to the design and steal both her fortune and her thunder. Catherine Littlefield Greene was never credited by Eli Whitney for her invaluable part in the invention of the cotton gin. Martha Coston's maritime signals are today known as "Very pistols" because a Lieutenant Very later made a small improvement on her device.

Some women were simply ahead of their time, or coincidentally working independently on the same subject as a more celebrated male researcher. Nettie Stevens's advances in genetics were overshadowed by identical discoveries made simultaneously by male colleagues in the scientific mainstream. Barbara McClintock saw her theories about "jumping genes" dismissed because they came thirty years too soon.

There are many others whom we would like to include here but, ironically, the forgotten women have been all but forgotten.

Catherine Littlefield Greene

COTTON GIN

Eli Whitney stands next to Thomas Alva Edison as the paragon of American ingenuity. Yet there is ample evidence to suggest that Whitney did not actually invent the cotton gin—or, at least, did not invent it without a good deal of assistance from southern belle Catherine Littlefield Greene, a heroine of the Revolutionary War and widow of General Nathaniel Greene.

Massachusetts-born Whitney was a guest in Mrs. Greene's Georgia home when he built his "cotton engine." Until that time, he probably had never so much as seen a raw cotton boll. It is commonly accepted that Whitney built his device after his hostess suggested that such a mechanism would be useful on the plantation. Some believe that Mrs. Greene actually presented Whitney with a complete set of drawings for her concept. At the very least, it is recorded that it was Catherine who approached a frustrated Whitney and hinted that his inoperable prototype might be improved by substituting wire teeth for the wooden ones he had built onto the gin's rollers. Her tactic not only worked, but also remains substantially unchanged some two hundred years later.

Catherine Greene never put her name on the cotton gin patent. It was just not the sort of thing a gentlewoman did in 1794. But she did share in the meager royalties received from the device, and she financed its manufacture by supporting the firm Whitney opened in partnership with her second husband, Phineas Miller. Because Whitney turned out to be a terrible businessman, Catherine never lost a potential fortune by forfeiting patent rights; she did, however, lose a place in history.

"Kitty" Littlefield was born in 1755 to a leading colonial family. She married Nathaniel Greene, thirteen years her senior and soon to become a trusted aide to General George Washington; their home was a center of Revolutionary society. Animated and flirtatious, Kitty also had a serious side: In 1777 she followed her husband to Valley Forge and spent the entire killing winter at his side.

Soon after the war, the Greenes settled down to plantation life on Mulberry Grove, the Georgia estate deeded Nathaniel by a grateful president. Within a year, Nathaniel was dead, leaving Catherine the house, the land, and five children.

The Eli Whitney connection came through Phineas Miller, a Connecticut native whom Catherine had hired to tutor her children. Miller eventually would become her second husband, but he was still only an employee when he met Whitney, a penniless tinkerer. Miller secured for his friend a teaching post at a nearby plantation, and when the job fell through, he brought Whitney home to Mulberry Grove.

Eli made himself useful around the house. He helped with the children and built Catherine a new embroidery frame. In the fall of 1792, he retired to the basement to try constructing the device Catherine spoke about: something to separate seeds from short-staple cotton and save hours of backbreaking labor by the family slaves.

Catherine supported Whitney for the six months he labored on the device (not ten days, as popular history has it), providing him with work space, tools, food, and ideas. When the gin was completed, she promoted the invention to neighboring plantation owners. Even if she did not actually hand over a complete set of plans, her contributions would have earned a partial patent assignment in ordinary situations. As it is, Whitney never so much as publicly thanked his patron.

By the time Eli Whitney got around to patenting his cotton gin officially (in partnership with Phineas Miller) in 1794, bootleg copies of the device were already in use throughout the South. Catherine Greene herself went broke financing Whitney's efforts to protect his rights in lengthy court battles. When she and Phineas Miller were married in 1796, the Whitney/Miller firm had managed to sell only six cotton gins. The company went out of business in 1797. The cotton gin became, as Whitney put it, "an invention . . . so valuable as to be worthless to the inventor."

It's ironic that Eli Whitney himself never profited from the cotton gin, as evidence suggests he may have claimed the credit unfairly. In 1807 he was refused an extension on his patent, and he never patented anything else before his death in 1825. Phineas Miller died of a fever in 1803 at age thirty-nine, leaving Catherine once again a widow. She moved her surviving family to a smaller estate, at Dungeness, Georgia, where she died—also of a fever—in 1814.

Lady Mary Montagu

SMALLPOX INOCULATION

Smallpox inoculation was introduced to Europe by Lady Mary Wortley Montagu, the outspoken intellectual diarist who is considered by some historians to be the first true feminist of Western civilization. Her application of a discovery she made in Turkey led to the first formulation of the germ theory of disease and saved the lives of countless millions who would have died of smallpox: In the British Isles alone, forty-five thousand people a year died of smallpox before her inoculations were introduced.

Of course, the discovery is almost universally credited to a male, Edward Jenner, who did basically the same experiment almost a century later. Jenner's 1798 research paper even established the term "vaccination."

But it was back in 1717 that Lady Mary and her husband, the British ambassador at Constantinople, traveled to Turkey. And, in April of that year, she wrote to a friend about the curious local custom called "ingrafting": "The small-pox, so fatal and so general amongst us, is here entirely harmless," she wrote. "Old women . . . make it their business to perform the operation every autumn . . . people send to one another to know if any of their family has a mind to have the small-pox: . . . the old woman comes with a nut-shell full of the matter of the . . . small-pox and asks what veins you please to have opened. She immediately rips open that you offer to her with a large needle." The result of this procedure, which most Westerners would have considered simply a bizarre tribal custom, was that the inoculated patients "keep to their beds two days, very seldom three . . . and in eight days' time they are as well as before." And immune from smallpox.

Lady Mary realized immediately the implications of this crude medical procedure, especially since she herself bore the scars of smallpox suffered in her youth. She also realized the obstacles against introducing it to England. "I should not fail to write some of our doctors very particularly about it," she noted, "if I knew any one of them that I thought had virtue enough to destroy such a considerable branch of their revenue for the good of mankind."

When she returned to England, Lady Mary had her own daughter inoculated against smallpox and got the approval of Caroline, Princess of Wales, to experiment with six convicts and six orphans to test the vaccinations. Then the princess's own daughters were inoculated. Despite vehement opposition from the med-

Iconoclastic Lady Mary Montagu brought back more than an outrageous fashion sense from her travels in the Middle East. She also introduced to the West the practice of variolation, precursor to modern vaccination and inoculation.

ical establishment and the Church, smallpox vaccination (or, more accurately when inoculating with a live virus, "variolation") took hold. Lady Mary published, anonymously, *Plain Account of the Inoculating of the Small-Pox by a Turkish Merchant* and lived to see the death rate from smallpox decrease from 30 percent mortality to 2 percent mortality.

Mary, great-granddaughter of Sir John Evelyn and niece of novelist Henry Fielding (who dedicated his first comedy to her), was a headstrong and unconventional young woman. In 1712 she eloped with Edward Wortley Montagu to spite her father, the earl of Kingston, who had arranged a marriage for her with an older man. A passionate reader in childhood, as an adult she became infamous for her witty correspondence (much of it with acidic poet Alexander Pope) and revelatory diaries. Today those diaries are considered some of the most important existing documents detailing life in the eighteenth century.

Lady Mary was described in her day as having "a tongue like a viper and a pen like a razor." She had literary success with her poetry, plays, and satires. *The Letters of Lady Mary Wortley Montagu* were most recently reprinted in 1965.

In 1736 Lady Mary created a sensation in Europe by leaving her husband for scientist Francesco Algarotti, who was twenty-three years her junior. She followed Algarotti to Italy, but he had moved on to Berlin after a summons from Frederick II. Lady Mary stayed in Venice to establish an intellectual salon on the Grand Canal, and she took up residence with young Count Ugo Palazzi. She returned to England in 1761, following the death of her husband, and died there a year later.

A monument was erected in the English Midlands town of Lichfield honoring Lady Mary's introduction of inoculation; a 1757 publication credited her alone with saving "many thousand British lives."

Martha J. Coston

MARITIME SIGNAL FLARES

For a woman who was left widowed and penniless—with three small children to support—at age twenty-one, Martha J. Coston realized some remarkable accomplishments in her life. She perfected and patented the signal flare conceived by her husband, and she singlehandedly marketed it in America and Europe. She walked with presidents, negotiated with generals, was entertained by royalty, traveled the world in grand style, and even lived to see her memoirs published (*A Signal Success,* by J. B. Lippincott Company, 1886). But her fondest wish in life never was granted. History still remembers the Coston signal light as the "Very pistol," named after Lieutenant E. W. Very, who made some minor re-finements to the signal's delivery system long after the device was in use. To her dying day Martha Coston wanted to see the Very name struck from the rolls and the name of Coston returned. In this she failed.

Martha Hunt—"Mattie" to her family and "Pattie" to her friends—was born in Baltimore in 1826, moving to Philadelphia when she was a child. At fourteen she eloped with Benjamin Cos-ton—all of nineteen himself, yet already a heralded inventor for his perfection of the "submarine torpedo," an underwater vessel that chemically manufactured its own oxygen supply. Assigned to a Washington, D.C., naval research lab, Benjamin moved his na-scent family (Martha was to have three sons in as many years) to the antebellum capital, where they participated in a privileged so-cial whirl.

After the birth of her fourth son, Martha's pleasant life was abruptly shattered: Benjamin caught cold on a business trip and was dead of pneumonia three months later. Within the year, the young widow also would lose her infant son and her mother to "the fever." On top of that, she learned that Benjamin's business partners and relatives had bankrupted his estate. In 1847 there was no Social Security or AFDC (Aid to Families with Dependent Children); Martha's options, as she saw them, were "to dig . . . or to beg," and she could do neither.

Distraught and bitter, she turned to her beloved Ben's me-mentos for solace—and found in an old trunk the plans for a pro-totype signal flare. This pyrotechnic cone would burn brightly in different colors, allowing ships to signal one another over distance and in fog or dark. Martha retrieved his models from the Navy, only to discover that they didn't work.

For almost a decade, the widow Coston—always wearing black—worked on perfecting the signal flares. She managed to get a bright white and a vivid red chemical fire, but she needed a third color to complete the standard maritime codes. "Blue I had my heart on," she wrote, "in order to use the national colors, but I could not obtain it with equal strength and intensity to the others."

It was while she watched a display celebrating the installation

of the Atlantic cable that Mrs. Coston got the idea of corresponding with fireworks manufacturers "under a man's name, fearing
they would not give heed to a woman." She eventually collaborated with one pyrotechnical chemist and succeeded in creating
not blue but green light.

Although she was not permitted to attend the Navy's tests of
her patents, Mrs. Coston did execute the government's order for
$6,000 worth of the flares and saw to it that she received addi-
tional patents for "Coston Telegraphic Night Signals" in England,
France, Holland, Austria, Denmark, Italy, and Sweden.

The Coston signal was instrumental in winning the Civil War
for the North: It enabled battleships to communicate strategic information over long distances, and it saved the lives of thousands
of seamen by preventing or pinpointing shipwrecks. Unfortunately for Coston Manufacturing Company, though, wartime in-
flation and government price ceilings meant that Martha was selling
her signals at a loss. Martha decided to market the device abroad.

Widow Coston never felt she received just compensation for
her revolutionary flare. When she asked $40,000 to turn over all
rights to the Union Congress, she got $20,000. She requested
$20,000 from the French government for patent rights, and they
gave $8,000. When, after the war, she was to get $21,000 in rep-
arations from the United States, she ended up with $13,000. Only
Denmark, she recalled, ever gave her what she considered fair market value.

"We hear much of the chivalry of men towards women," she
wrote, "but let me tell you, gentle reader, it vanishes like dew
before the summer sun when one of us comes into competition
with the manly sex. . . . It was a most bitter thing to find in that
lofty institution of our country, the Navy, men so small-minded
that they begrudged a woman her success."

Later in life, Mrs. Coston spent many years traveling through
Europe, Russia, and Scandinavia. She never remarried, although
she was briefly engaged to an Italian count. (Before the wedding
he died, which Martha claimed was a murder plot by his relatives
who didn't want her to inherit his title and fortune.) During the
French Revolution, she carried her case of sample signal flares la-

beled as a music box, lest she be accused of spying.

Two of the Coston children grew to adulthood: William devised a series of color codes widely used by the merchant marine and private yachts; Harry became manager of the manufacturing facility, and he invented a pistol system for firing the Coston flares, which were traditionally hand-held. It was for an improvement to the cartridge for this pistol that Lieutenant Very received his patent and to whom history has given the lion's share of inventor's credit. "In silence," Martha wrote, "I was obliged to see my signal used in the U.S. Navy under the name of the Very signal."

Madame Lefebre

FERTILIZER

The conversion of airborne nitrogen gas into nitrate fertilizers was a staple of agribusiness by the 1920s; existing nitrate deposits (mostly in South America) could no longer provide the millions of tons of nitrogen fertilizers that were needed for worldwide soil enhancement. But it was more than fifty years earlier that the process for fixing nitrogen gas into fertilizer was invented, and its inventor never received credit for her contribution. Even her given name has been lost to the history books.

Madame Lefebre, a Parisian, patented the process for making nitrates out of nitrogen gas as early as 1859. The patent was granted in England and was totally ignored. At the time, the world was a lifetime away from the stage when the American cotton crop alone would require three million tons of fertilizer annually. The idea fell into a void, and when it was resuscitated half a century later, others received the accolades and remuneration that were Mme. Lefebre's due.

Nettie M. Stevens

X AND Y CHROMOSOMES

Nettie Stevens's career was something of an oddity. Unlike most intellectual women of her era, she was not a fiery youngster driven with scholastic ambition. Born in 1861 in Vermont, Nettie worked as a schoolmarm and a librarian, and waited until she was in her thirties to go to college—although one family genealogist contends that, contrary to accepted reports, she may have enrolled as early as age twenty. Either way, it was definitely in 1896 that she enrolled at Stanford, which made her a thirty-five-year-old freshman.

Nettie graduated in 1899 and earned her master's degree in physiology a year later. Having published her first scientific paper, a study of protozoan life cycles, in 1901, she moved back East to take her Ph.D. at Bryn Mawr and would spend the bulk of her career there as a professor.

In 1905 Dr. Stevens published a monograph that identified the X and Y chromosomes and pinpointed their role in determining the sex of an embryo: the XX combination produces a female, and the XY a male. Similar work on the subject of sex determination was being conducted independently—and simultaneously—by one of Stevens's former colleagues, Edmund B. Wilson. But he couldn't or wouldn't be as specific as Stevens in defining these actual X and Y chromosomes.

One could hardly blame Wilson—who is, of course, the scientist now commonly credited with Stevens's discovery—for his reticence in pinpointing gender inheritance. In a society based on male superiority and primogeniture, it was much more convenient to suppose—as everyone did—that fathers contribute maleness and mothers contribute femaleness, the outcome ordained by divine intervention. The X and Y theory meant that it was the *father* who "allowed" the birth of a daughter, by virtue of having contributed his X chromosome.

Nettie Stevens, a self-effacing woman more interested in her teaching than her reputation as a scientist, never bullied the establishment into accepting her theories. She was honored by her colleagues and beloved by her students, and she continued to study with renowned geneticists worldwide. After Stevens's death in 1912 from breast cancer, Wilson continued the research into gender inheritance and eventually duplicated and confirmed her findings. Today Nettie Stevens isn't even mentioned in the multivolume *Dictionary of Scientific Biography*.

Rosalind Franklin

DNA

Microchemist Rosalind Franklin went through her scientific life with a chip on her shoulder, and it's no wonder. Even though she was the first researcher to discern the complex structure of the DNA (deoxyribonucleic acid) molecule, her colleagues wouldn't so much as let her in their meetings to discuss her findings. Instead, they cavalierly took her papers and handed them around to her competition. After all, Miss Franklin was invading an all-male scientific establishment and to complicate matters, she was Jewish.

It was Rosalind Franklin who was the integral fourth team member—with Maurice Wilkins, James Watson, and Francis Crick—responsible for the discovery of the famed "double helix." That she wasn't a corecipient of the 1962 Nobel Prize that the trio shared was a tragic irony: Franklin died of cancer in 1958, and the Nobel Prize goes only to living people. That her contributions continued to be denigrated by her colleagues (James Watson referred to her as "Rosy" in his 1968 book *The Double Helix* and implied that she was little more than a lab assistant) is shameful. In fact, Rosalind Franklin was the first person, back in 1951, to deduce the helical structure of DNA; she even showed Watson the fundamental error in his first double-helix model and put him on the track to his prizewinning findings.

Rosalind Franklin always made life difficult for herself. Born in 1920 into a socially prominent Jewish banking family in London, she disappointed her parents by heading for a scientific career instead of a philanthropical one. When she graduated from Newnham College at Cambridge in 1941, she was awarded a research scholarship to work under Ronald Norrish (who would win the Nobel Prize himself in 1967)—a man who resented her very presence and fought her every step of the way. Franklin relocated to the Central Laboratory of Chemical Sciences in Paris, where she made important discoveries in crystallography and molecular structure, and returned to work at King's College in London. There she again found herself supervised by a scientist who considered her an affront. Maurice Wilkins refused to accept female doctoral candidates under his direction as late as the 1970s, and between 1951 and 1953 he was known to have turned Franklin's findings—without her permission—over to his friends Watson and Crick.

Although she published a breakthrough paper on the structure of DNA in 1953, and although her X-ray photographs were used by Watson as vital evidence in his grant application, Franklin became so frustrated with the treatment she was receiving that she left King's College in 1953. She took a research position at Birkbeck College instead, where she delineated important findings about virus particles. While at Birkbeck, she was forbidden to talk about

DNA, although her work in virology contributed significantly to the understanding of genetics. She mounted an exhibition at the 1958 World's Fair in Brussels at the behest of the Royal Society, but this official recognition was both too little and too late. In that same year, she learned she had incurable cancer.

Always a loner, Franklin told none of her coworkers that she was in pain; she asked for no sympathy, and she received none. She continued to work until her death at age thirty-seven, dying a bitter and frustrated woman. Unhappily, history has proved her distrust of her colleagues, and there is no upbeat footnote to Rosalind Franklin's life. Her scientific contributions were unrecognized when she lived and remain unrecognized after her death.

Barbara McClintock

''JUMPING GENES''

In 1951 geneticist Barbara McClinock discovered that everyone was wrong about genes and chromosomes. The scientific establishment said that genes—those basic building blocks of information in every cell—are attached to chromosomes in a strict, linear fashion. "Like pearls on a string," they explained it. People wanted to believe that, as Mendel had demonstrated with his generations of peas, inherited characteristics are predictable and logical. No one wanted to hear Dr. McClintock's heretical theory that genes "jump," that they indulge in random behavior, and that they can even pass from cell to cell.

"They thought I was quite mad," said Dr. McClintock. In twenty years, she noted, only three people requested to see a copy of her paper on the phenomenon.

When Dr. Barbara McClintock won the Nobel Prize in Medicine and Physiology in 1983, the award committee said it was no surprise that these theories had been rejected for decades. "Only about five geneticists in the world could appreciate them," stated a committee member, "because of the complexity of the work." Once established as genetic dogma, Dr. McClintock's discovery made it possible to study antibiotic-resistant bacteria, to seek a cure for African sleeping sickness, and to make inroads in defusing the cancer mechanism. It was "one of the two great discoveries of our time in genetics," said the Nobel spokesman.

"When you know you're right," said Dr. McClintock with a shrug, "you don't care what other people think. You know sooner or later it will come out in the wash."

Barbara McClintock formulated her unpopular theories by watching generation after generation of Indian corn. For fifty years she worked alone in her Long Island, New York, patch of maize, never even employing a lab assistant. Painfully shy, the petite (five-foot, one-hundred-pound) scientist said she was perfectly content with her monastic life. When she won the Nobel Prize, she only learned the news from a radio broadcast, since she possessed no telephone. And, at age eighty-one, she saw no reason to change any lifetime habits simply because she had just earned $190,000.

Barbara McClintock was born on June 16, 1902, in Hartford, Connecticut, and divided her early years between New England and New York City. Her father was a doctor, but that didn't mean her mother approved of advanced education . . . for girls. It was over Mother's protests that Barbara enrolled at Cornell University in 1919. She intended to study plant breeding, but the department wouldn't admit any women. She majored instead in botany, and she turned to plant genetics while working toward her 1927 doctorate.

Women—even Ph.D. women—were forbidden to hold tenured professorships in the 1930s, and Dr. McClintock's reputation as a loner and a maverick earned her a few dismissals in those years. In 1942 she was outright unemployed. If it hadn't been for the encouragement of a former colleague from Cornell, her life might have gone very differently. As it was, Marcus Rhoades helped her land a research grant from the Carnegie Institute, which set her up in a modest botanical facility at Cold Spring Harbor on Long Island's North Shore. And then Carnegie did the best thing McClintock could have wished for: They left her alone.

Until she broke ranks in 1951, McClintock's studies in genetics were widely honored. In 1944 she became the third woman ever elected to the National Academy of Sciences and said in her acceptance speech, "I am not a feminist, but I am always gratified when illogical barriers are broken—for Jews, women, Negroes, etc. It helps us all."

After her breakthrough findings were announced—and roundly denounced—Dr. McClintock stopped publishing her papers: No one read them, and no one believed them. She worked in virtual obscurity ten and twelve hours a day, thankful that Carnegie (through some oversight, she supposed) never fired her. Finally the science of genetics caught up with her.

In 1981 McClintock won the Albert Lasker Basic Medical Research Award, worth $15,000. Later in the same year she received $50,000 from the Israel Wolf Foundation and shortly thereafter was granted an annuity of $60,000 a year (tax-free) for life by the MacArthur Foundation. She used the newfound wealth to indulge herself in two "extravagances": a Japanese car and a new pair of eyeglasses.

When she won the Nobel Prize, Dr. McClintock consented to only one press conference. She never crowed about her overdue vindication; she never held a grudge. "It might seem unfair," she even said, "to reward a person for having so much pleasure over the years. I can't imagine having a better life."

Jocelyn Bell

THE PULSAR

In 1974 Antony Hewish, professor of astronomy at the Cambridge University, received the Nobel Prize in physics "for his decisive role in the discovery of pulsars." Not a word was mentioned during the awards ceremony that it was Hewish's graduate student, Jocelyn Bell, who actually made the discovery in 1967.

The pulsating star, or pulsar, that Bell discovered was an entirely new celestial phenomenon. In the scheme of astronomy, which is man's oldest science, the discovery still is too new to determine all its ramifications, but many believe pulsars may hold clues to the beginnings of the universe.

Born in 1943 in York, England, Bell was only twenty-four years old when she made her amazing find. As a research student, she specialized in radio astronomy, which uses giant radarlike dishes to detect electromagnetic waves from outside the earth's atmosphere. She was permitted to use the 4.5-acre radio dish at Cambridge, which produced weekly data amounting to some four hundred feet of recorder chart paper.

In August 1967 she was looking for "interstellar scintillation"—pulsating, celestial radio sources that had previously been observed—when she began to notice some strange signals coming in during the dead of night, when scintillation normally was the weakest. For the next three months the signals disappeared and reappeared—until November, when she used a high-speed recorder that revealed that the signals pulsated on a regular interval of just over a second. All other celestial radio signals previously recorded emitted a constant signal.

When Bell's discovery was made public in 1968, no one had a definitive explanation for the phenomenon, although theories ran rampant. Some suggested that this was the long-awaited sign from our alien cousins. Eventually, the theory proposed by Franco Pacini and Thomas Gold became accepted: Pulsars are rapidly rotating neutron stars—stars consisting entirely of neutron particles resulting from the collapse of a much larger star.

No one has ever seen a pulsar, since they are detectable only by the pulsating radio signals they emit, but more than three hundred have been recorded since Bell's initial discovery. Some pulsars have such an extraordinarily rapid and uniform "pulse" that scientists are beginning to use them as intergalactic clocks. One day soon, scientists will be able to determine if pulsars are moving away or toward the earth, an important clue in discovering the age and origin of the universe.

While Hewish, Bell's immediate supervisor, was instrumental in subsequent research on pulsars, the Nobel Foundation simply chose to ignore the well-documented fact that his assistant was the first to identify the source of the pulsating radio signals.

Bell completed her Ph.D. in 1968 and now works as a research fellow at the Mullard Space Science Laboratory at University College in London.

Carrie J. Everson

ORE EXTRACTION

Women were a rarity in the mining communities of the Old West—
to such an extent that one could literally make a fortune during
the Gold Rush by taking in washing. There were a few hearty
female souls digging away at their dreams (almost a hundred women
emigrated to Alaska in 1900 to mine the Klondike), but the majority of women settlers in the gold country were wives or tem-
porary-wives-for-hire. One notable exception was Carrie J. Everson,
who moved to Colorado as a schoolteacher and ended up as a
heroine to miners by inventing the process that separates precious
metal from dross. Her oil flotation system, patented in 1886, was
the basis of modern mining separation processes.

Carrie Everson moved from Chicago to Colorado along with
her brother, an assayer, and helped him out when she wasn't in
the classroom. When she was washing out a dirty, greasy ore sack,
she noticed the iron pyrite ("fool's gold") floated in the oily water,
while the gold flakes settled to the bottom.

Everson conducted lengthy experiments in oil separation and
the acid-wash process that would extract the purified metals. "I
have used petroleum in its several constituents," she wrote, "also
tallow, lard, cotton-seed oil, castor oil and linseed-oil. The acids
which I have employed are sulphuric, hydrochloric, nitric, phos-
phoric, acetic, oxalic, tannic and gallic." She discovered that her
process was effective for low-quality, rocky ores containing gold,
silver, iron, copper, sulfur, and antimony. "Its commercial value,

however," she noted, "will probably be restricted to its use in connection with ores bearing the precious metals, such as gold, silver and copper."

The Everson patent was a landmark in mining; yet if anyone were to be asked to list influential women from the Gold Rush era, few could get beyond dancers Lola Montez and Lotta Crabtree or "unsinkable" Molly Brown. The woman who made untold fortunes for others has been all but forgotten.

Celebrity Inventors

SOME WOMEN were made famous by their inventions; some women were famous despite them. The desire to invent suffuses both *le monde et le demi-monde*—who would have thought that sensuous actress Hedy Lamarr would have patented a secret wartime communication system (of all things) under her given name of Hedwig Kiesler Markey? There are aristocratic inventors (Lady Ada Lovelace, Lady Montagu, who can be found in the "Unsung Heroines" chapter, and Countess Stella Andrassy, who can be found in the section on solar engineering), and there are inventors who found fame on stage and screen. In almost every case, their celebrity outlasted their inventing acclaim, but that does not make them any less inventors.

Lady Ana de Osorio

QUININE

It was the countess of Chinchon, vicereine of Peru, who introduced the cure for malaria to Europe. Chinchona bark, named for her, produced the quinine that was to become the most important medical advance of the seventeenth century.

While serving in Lima, Peru, Spanish Countess Ana de Osorio was treated for "tertian fever" in 1638. She brought a supply of the miraculous bark back to Spain with her and introduced its curative powers to the medical establishment. Quinine was known for centuries as *pulvis comitessa*—the countess's powder. The name chinchona has since been Anglicized to cinchona, and few remember the royal lady who brought it to Europe.

Lady Ada Lovelace

COMPUTER FORERUNNER

Lady Ada Lovelace was the only legitimate child of the doomed romantic poet Lord Byron, the issue of a short and unhappy marriage. Ada was, by all accounts, a spoiled, self-important, whimsical woman. She probably was a hypochrondriac, definitely a compulsive gambler, and apparently drug-dependent for much of her life. She was also, most likely, a mathematical genius. Alongside inventor George Babbage, Ada worked on the chimeral "analytical engine," a mechanical device that would do complex calculations. It was she who first arrived at the concept of "programming," and—although the crude technology of the day kept an analytical engine from actually being constructed in her lifetime—today there is a military computer programming language called ADA in her honor.

Ada Byron was born in 1815, a "sickly child" whose domineering mother both cosseted her and subjected her to frequent leechings and bloodletting. (Later in life, Lady Byron would dose her daughter with prescriptives of laudanum—tincture of heroin, basically—and create serious psychological damage as well.) Ada was tutored at home in mathematics, astronomy, Latin, and music, and established correspondence with notable British scientists to broaden her knowledge.

Ada Lovelace had first made the acquaintance of the mathematical engineer George Babbage in 1834, and she began immersing herself in the fields of calculus and analysis. Her published

Lady Ada Lovelace, only legitimate child of tragic poet Lord Byron, helped design the prototype Analytical Engine, grandmother of today's computers.

commentaries on L. F. Menabrea's theories were admired as containing as much—or more—abstract mathematical analysis than the original, Italian document.

George Babbage had the idea of a "difference engine" (one that could add and subtract) long before he met Ada, and he devised the "analytical engine" (a legitimate precursor to the computer) without her assistance. But it was Ada who first designed the punch-card programs that would instruct the analytical engine in its tasks. It was she who conceptualized what this day and age refers to as the law of GIGO: Garbage In, Garbage Out.

"The Analytical Engine has no pretensions whatever to originate anything," wrote Ada in 1843. "It can do whatever we know how to order it to perform. It can follow analysis; but it has no power to anticipating any analytical relationships or truths."

Although some £17,000 of public funds were spent by Babbage to create a working model of his engine (not to mention his personal fortune and, probably, some of Ada's), the tools of the era weren't up to the task. Fighting such roadblocks as denial of permission to use the Royal Society's library (no women allowed), Ada herself continued to study the nascent science of cybernetics and once wrote that she hoped "to bequeath to future generations a Calculus of the Nervous System." She was no more successful than Babbage.

At a low point in her life, Lady Ada Lovelace developed chronic asthma and became tied to the laudanum and morphine that were being used to treat her. She also became hooked on gambling, feeling that an astute enough mathematical system—one she was sure she was capable of devising—could beat the racetrack odds. She never did, and the attempt to prove her theories cost her much of her fortune.

By the end of her life, Ada had overcome her need for medication, although the urge to gamble never left her. She became ever more sickly, now due to the cancer that would prove terminal. She died in 1852 at age thirty-six.

Lillian Russell

DRESSER-TRUNK

Lillian Russell, superstar of the Gay Nineties' musical theater, took her show on the road in grand style. She had a personal Pullman railcar, dubbed *The Iolanthe,* and traveled thousands of miles a year surrounded by velvet couches, gold tassels, and the sparks and ash of a wood-burning stove. To make the traveling life a little more convenient, Miss Russell designed a custom dresser-trunk for her own use and had it patented in 1912. The device, she explained, "will answer to all the requirements of an actress . . . and can be used by the traveling public and by campers."

The dresser-trunk—never a commercial success due to its complexity—was a series of drawers, lights, hooks, brackets, hinges, and mirrors that folded into themselves for easy shipping. Russell designed it to have "all the cosmetics and necessities of a 'make-up' at hand, and with the mirrors and lighting fixtures so arranged that the desired results could be quickly accomplished, as is nec-

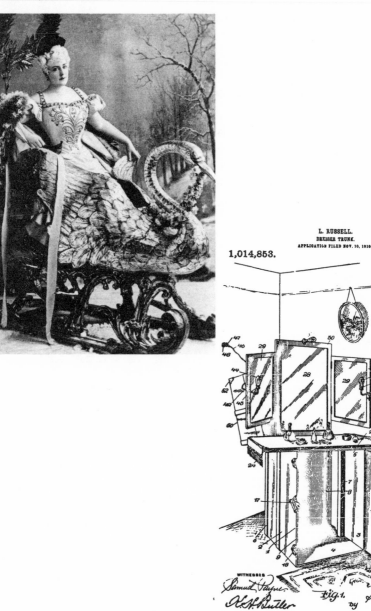

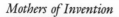

Gay Nineties archetype Lillian Russell (shown here in one of her more flamboyant productions) had so much trouble transporting her cumbersome costumes and makeup kits that she patented a special dresser trunk to do the job more efficiently.

essary when the interval between acts is very short.

"Furthermore," she continued in her patent application, "it is extremely important that a trunk of the above type will withstand the rough usage to which it is subjected when being carried on a theatrical tour, therefore it has been made very rigid and durable."

"Rigid and durable" might be used to describe the inventor as much as the invention in this case. Lillian Russell survived four marriages, World War I, scandal, and luxury to become the best-paid performer of her day. In 1891 she was earning $1,200 a week plus a percentage of the box office at T. Henry French's Manhattan Garden Theatre—a sum that would support a small city, much less a large family, in its time. Her beauty and singing voice were legendary, and she was an astute businesswoman without spoiling her image as an ideal of femininity.

Lillian Russell was born Helen Louise Leonard in Clinton, Iowa, on December 4, 1861. By 1890 her work in musical comedy and light opera was world-renowned; she was asked, in fact, to be the first voice ever heard on a long-distance telephone. Adored for her beauty as well as her talent, she lent her name (not her formulas) to "Lillian Russell's Own Preparation," a line of cosmetics, and she was poster girl for the Marine Corps recruiting campaign.

By the end of her life, Russell became more involved in intellectual pursuits. At age fifty she got a job as a newspaper columnist, and in 1922 President Harding appointed her special investigator on immigration problems. She died that year, at age sixty, of heart failure, never regretting the one career failure of her life— the nonacceptance of the Russell Dresser-Trunk.

Hedy Lamarr

SECRET COMMUNICATION SYSTEM

In her steamy autobiography *Ecstasy and Me,* silver-screen siren Hedy Lamarr breathlessly writes that her only contribution to the Allied effort during World War II was her "cocoa-butter-smeared nudity" as Tondelayo in the movie *White Cargo.* That's what she would like you to believe.

In reality she and composer George Antheil—one of the few male friends Hedy never married, it seems—invented a classified communications system especially suitable for submarines, for which they received Patent No. 2,292,387 on June 10, 1941. The invention in theory was quite ingenious, utilizing a system whereby the radio frequencies would change intermittently and simultaneously between the transmitter and receiver in order to defeat enemy monitoring of the signals. However, since not one military history so much as hints that such a device ever was used, one can assume that practice and theory didn't match up.

The reason Lamarr chose to keep such an achievement secret all these years probably has to do with the actress's perception of her public image. In the Golden Age of Hollywood, image was all-important and, even today, Lamarr is extremely sensitive about the way the public sees her. She filed an injunction against a national tabloid in 1986 to block the publication of an unflattering photo of herself.

Born Hedwig Kiesler in 1913, 1914 or 1915 (depending on which account you read), she began her film career with a splash—liter-

Who would guess that this femme fatale would patent a secret World War II communications system? Hedy Lamarr never publicly acknowledges the patent, but then she was the only Hedwig Kiesler Markey around in 1941.

"Why don't you pick one up and smoke it sometime?" crooned TV star Edie Adams in her Muriel Cigar campaign. And to make the task easier, she invented a cigar holder disguised as a ring.

ally. Her first starring role was in a 1933 Czech film, *Ecstasy,* during which the still teenaged Lamarr is shown frolicking in a pond completely nude. Banned in Boston (and everywhere else in the United States), it nevertheless caught the attention of Louis B. Mayer, head of MGM, who—against his better judgment—signed the Lolita-like ingenue to a contract.

In retrospect, it's not difficult to see what swayed the normally conservative Mayer. Lamarr was exquisite, already being talked about, in some quarters, as the next Garbo. In 1938 Miss Kiesler made her American film debut as Hedy Lamarr in *Algiers*—playing the part of the ravishing brunette to whom Charles Boyer offered moviedom's most famous invitation: "Come with me to the Casbah."

This was the first and last film of any critical note that Lamarr ever made. MGM's answer to Paramount's Dorothy Lamour, Hedy was cast in one B-flick after another (*Lady of the Tropics,* 1939; *Ziegfeld Girl,* 1941; *Tortilla Flat* and *White Cargo,* 1942; *Her Highness and the Bellboy,* 1944; and so on). Her limited roles cannot entirely be blamed on MGM, however. Twice she had screen immortality in her grasp—but she turned down the roles that would make Ingrid Bergman famous in *Casablanca* (1943) and *Gaslight* (1944).

By the end of the war, Hedy's Hollywood salad days were long withered—although in 1950 her starring role opposite Victor Mature in Cecil B. DeMille's *Samson and Delilah* helped to make it the biggest box office draw of the year. In 1954 her beauty was still sufficient to make her a believable Helen of Troy in the Italian feature film *The Face That Launched a Thousand Ships.* Her last film was *The Female Animal* in 1957.

Even in the liberated 1980s, Hedy Lamarr refuses to admit that she had a secret identity as a technologist. She will not be interviewed on the subject (although she's vocal about other topics, like her sex life) and has never publicly confirmed that the Hedwig Kiesler Markey on the 1941 patent is the same Hedwig "Hedy" Kiesler (a.k.a. Lamarr) who was married to screenwriter Gene Markey at the time. Perhaps her need to see herself as the quintessential "female animal" keeps her from admitting that she ever was a closet intellectual.

Edie Adams

CIGAR HOLDER-RING

For almost two decades, Edie Adams and Muriel cigars were inseparable in the public mind. When she cooed, "Why don't you pick one up and smoke it sometime," she created one of the more memorable advertising campaigns on television. And in many of those ads, millions of viewers got a rare look at an invention she herself patented—an invention that was manufactured by a diamond jeweler and used only by Miss Adams and a few of her close friends. The cigar holder-ring, which she designed in 1963, was just one example of Adams's philosophy: "Anytime anyone tells me something's as good as it gets, I look for seven ways to do it better."

The idea for the cigar holder-ring came when the Muriel company was trying to make cigars more palatable to women. "I said to them, 'There's no way you're going to get me to hold a big fat cigar,'" recalls Adams. "And then I remembered seeing Gloria Swanson, I believe it was in *Sunset Boulevard,* with an odd cigarette holder. I wondered if there was a way to make something similar for cigars, constructing it as a one-piece device instead of requiring two or three pieces."

By twisting a piece of wire, Adams came up with a springlike device that adjusted easily for both the size of the index finger it would slip around and the width of the cigar that would slip into it. "It was the economy of the design, the fact that it was all one piece, that made it worth patenting," says Adams. "Muriel was going to pursue it further, so I had Cartier make up a couple of prototypes. I never made any money from the invention, though, because right around then even men stopped smoking cigars."

A classically trained singer, Adams—*née* Edith Adams Enke— first exhibited a talent for design as a teenager, remodeling hand-me-downs. Her career as a comedienne reached its height during the "golden age of television," when she costarred with husband Ernie Kovacs in his landmark variety series. Her own TV shows included *Here's Edie, The Edie Adams Show,* and she appeared in such popular films as *The Apartment* and *Lover Come Back.*

Miss Adams hardly considers the invention of a cigar holder-ring a highlight of her life but is proud that it exemplifies her altogether inventive mind. "I'm driven to improving things," she says. "I'm learning to cook right now, and there are a lot of standard things in the kitchen that I just know could use improvement." Asked what she would most want to invent, Edie Adams replies: "A peace program that works."

Dorothy Rodgers

THE JONNY MOP

Cleaning toilet bowls isn't romantic, but someone has to do it. And inventing a tool for cleaning toilet bowls may not be very romantic, either, but somebody had to do that, too. Interestingly, it was a woman with a very romantic aura who invented the Jonny Mop toilet cleaner: Dorothy Rodgers, wife of composer Richard Rodgers, whose credits include the lavish musicals *South Pacific, The King and I, Carousel,* and *The Sound of Music.*

Mrs. Rodgers patented the plastic-handled contrivance with the flushable cleaning head in 1945. "I thought there just had to be a better way to scrub toilets than the old-fashioned, unsanitary brush method," she said. She sold her rights to a manufacturer for $10,000 plus royalties and then had to sue the firm later when they tried to withhold her proceeds. (They claimed to have changed the original design enough so that Dorothy's patent no longer protected her; the courts disagreed.)

Aside from the Jonny Mop and its patented improvement, the Tank-U, Dorothy Rodgers invented the Try-On Dress Pattern (which could be washed, ironed, and altered) and an educational game for children called the Turn and Learn Books.

Beatrix Potter

LICHEN

Beatrix Potter is well known as the creator of Peter Rabbit and scores of beloved children's stories. She is less well known as the discoverer of lichen, the first person to identify the common growth as not a variety of plant at all, but rather as a symbiotic relationship between algae and fungi. The fact that she described this scientific phenomenon ten years before it was accepted botanical theory is all but unknown today, because Potter was so frustrated by the cold shoulder she got from the scientific establishment that she totally abandoned her studies. She left behind only a series of carefully encoded notebooks—which wouldn't be deciphered until half a century later.

Beatrix Potter was born in 1866 to an upper-class British family. She was raised by a governess who taught her the usual French, German, and needlework, but by age twelve Beatrix was showing a remarkable talent for drawing. Her father was what we would now call a "celebrity photographer," and young Beatrix often accompanied him on shoots.

As a teenager, Beatrix would spend time in the woods, studying fungi and lichen and making intricate drawings of her subjects. When she determined that the lichen she observed were actually a synthesis of two other life forms, she went to her uncle, Sir Henry Roscoe, a noted chemist. He encouraged her work, and he took her to the Royal Botanical Gardens to present her ideas to the director, Sir William Thistleton-Dyer. Thistleton-Dyer took one look at her papers and said they were "too artistic to be scientific."

Twice more Miss Potter tried to gain the ear of Thistleton-Dyer, only to be rebuffed. Sir Henry continued to support her efforts, however, and saw to it that her paper on symbiosis was read (by a male assistant) at the Linnaean Society in 1897, where it was accepted as a scientific breakthrough. Instead of publishing her findings, however, Beatrix took the paper back and hid it from the world.

She turned then to children's literature and became a successful, respected author and illustrator. Potter died in England in 1943.

Herschel / Lavoisier / Pasteur / Brahe / Hall

SISTERS AND SPOUSES

Many inventions and discoveries credited to men were made in partnership with—or with the invaluable assistance of—either their wives or their sisters. Few of these women ever received recognition for their participation.

One who is generally known for her work both as a helpmate and as an individual is German astronomer Caroline Herschel. Born in Hanover in 1750, Caroline moved to England at age twenty-two and gave up a budding singing career to work as assistant to her brother, William, in his studies of astronomy.

William Herschel discovered the planet Uranus in 1781 and became a respected scientist of his day. He was appointed king's astronomer to George III at a salary of £200 a year, and Caroline herself was voted £50 a year salary as his assistant—after having done the job gratis for six years.

Caroline Herschel not only kept house for her brother, she also hand-fed him when he was absorbed in his observations and read to him so he wouldn't go crazy. In addition, she stayed up all night making detailed observation sweeps of the skies; made the models and mirrors for the custom-built forty-foot telescope that Herschel needed for his work; and constructed the molds for the telescope mirrors herself—by pounding bushels of horse manure through a giant sieve.

In 1782 William gave his sister a small telescope of her own so she could make personal observations and calculations. Her earliest independent discoveries included three new nebulae, and by the time a year was out she had discovered several new star clusters and fourteen more nebulae. On August 1, 1786, she became the first woman ever recognized for discovering a comet, something William himself never achieved. By 1797 Caroline had discovered a total of eight comets. Her first was seen by the naked eye in Paris during January 1790.

Caroline and William Herschel are credited with establishing the science of sidereal astronomy. They not only increased the size of telescopes but also designed optical improvements and invented methods of mounting and casting them. Caroline's life work was *A Catalogue of the Nebulae,* which listed the positions of twenty-five hundred star systems and was not completed until she was seventy-five years old. (With typical self-effacement, Caroline subtitled the volume *Which Have Been Observed by William Herschel,* never crediting her own nights of star sweeps.)

Miss Herschel received the Gold Medal of the Royal Astronomical Society in 1828, an honor she greeted with mixed emotion. "Throughout my long-spent life, I have not been used or had any desire of having public honours bestowed on me," she wrote to her nephew, astronomer John Herschel.

In 1836 Caroline was elected to the Royal Irish Academy and in 1846 was awarded the Gold Medal for Science by the king of Prussia. She continued to study science and correspond with other researchers in her field well into her nineties, even though she was functionally blind by that time. She died in 1848 at age ninety-seven.

Antoine Lavoisier got his name in the schoolbooks of the ages by identifying the element oxygen, correcting long-held misconceptions about the alchemical substance phlogiston. Less honored is his collaborator, Marie Anne Peirrette Paulze, who married Lavoisier in 1772. She was then fourteen years old.

Lavoisier was already twenty-eight and an established chemist when Marie married him to escape an unpleasant, prearranged marriage to an even older man. She entered the union with gusto, setting about to learn Latin and English to translate foreign texts for her husband. She assisted with all his experiments, took all the notes, kept the laboratory records, and carried on the couple's scientific correspondence with other researchers.

In 1783 Lavoisier announced his theory of combustion, and Marie dramatically burned all their texts containing the old phlogiston theories. She illustrated the 1789 volume of *Traite de Chimie*, considered to be the first modern chemistry text.

Antoine Lavoisier was executed on the guillotine in 1794 for the crime of being an aristocrat during the French Revolution. Marie became a fugitive from the Reign of Terror and was briefly imprisoned herself. Her father was guillotined, and her estates were confiscated (although subsequently restored). In 1805 Marie Lavoisier published "*Mémoires de Chimie*," the completion of an eight-volume work that Antoine had only dented. She published it under his name.

That same year, Marie remarried, to American Tory scientist Count Rumford, but they separated before 1810. She established a reputation as an astute businesswoman and a philanthropist, but she died in 1836 regretful that her gender kept her from continuing any serious scientific study on her own.

Marie Laurent worked closely with Louis Pasteur after their marriage in 1849. Mme. Pasteur was a close collaborator with her husband throughout his research, both working in the lab and writing papers. She was his number one assistant and can legitimately be credited as codiscoverer of the rabies vaccine. In 1868 Pasteur became paralyzed, and Marie supervised all the lab's experiments from that date forward.

Tycho Brahe has a piece of the moon named for him, but the honor should be shared with Sofie Brahe, his sister. Self-taught astronomer and alchemist Sofie was born about 1556, and she worked alongside Tycho at the Uraniborg Observatory throughout his career. She died in 1643.

In more recent history, it is necessary to credit Julia B. Hall as coinventor of aluminum manufacture with her brother, Charles Martin Hall. Charles Hall's 1886 invention of a cheap method for producing aluminum led to the establishment of the multimillion-dollar Alcoa (Aluminum Company of America) from its forerunner, the Pittsburgh Reduction Company, for which Julia held a hundred shares of original stock. As Charles's older sister, she saved the patent rights to Charles's invention and made possible the family fortune.

Julia Brainerd Hall was born November 11, 1859, to a missionary family living in the British West Indies. She was an infant when her parents returned to Ohio, and her four younger sisters and two younger brothers were born and raised there. All the Hall siblings graduated from Oberlin College, a most unusual situation in the era.

Although the "Ladies' Course" at Oberlin tended more toward liberal arts and veered away from hard science, Julia Hall did receive a solid background in chemistry, geology, economics, and mathematics. In fact, she had more science credits upon receiving her degree (not diploma; women weren't allowed them) than her brother. When she graduated in 1881, she took up housekeeping for her sick mother, who died in 1885.

Charles conducted his first experiments in the woodshed behind the Hall residence during the years 1882–86. Julia was in the lab every day taking careful notes on his work and offering suggestions. After Charles left the household, the pair continued to correspond on his researches, and it was Julia's careful note-taking and saving of letters that made possible Charles's patent defense against the Frenchman Heroult, who claimed priority over Hall's discovery. Thanks to Julia, Charles M. Hall would earn $170,000 a year from Alcoa stock by the time of his death in 1914, and he was able to leave $3 million to Oberlin alone. Julia herself received some $7,000 a year from her stock by that time.

Julia never married, continuing to care for her father until he died at age eighty-eight. Documentation of Julia's own life becomes obscure after the death of her brother, who was her link to fame in a world that cared little for an elderly spinster.

APPENDIX 1

The Women's Bureau

ON JUNE 5, 1920, in the wake of the ratification of the constitutional amendment giving women the right to vote, Congress ordered that a Women's Bureau be established within the Department of Labor: "It shall be the duty of said bureau to formulate standards and policies, which shall promote the welfare of wage-earning women, improve their working conditions, increase their efficiency and advance their opportunities for profitable employment."

With a feminist named Mary Anderson at its helm, the bureau undertook to study how "women [have] made material contributions to the sum total of creative achievements." They picked a period—1905–21—during which 5,016 patents were granted to women.

The statistical analysis was startling. Women had patented not one or a dozen but hundreds of innovations in "men's" fields, such as agriculture, mining, ordnance and firearms, masonry and construction, automobile engineering, electrical equipment, power machinery, laboratory equipment, optical and photographic goods, and industrial safety equipment. Household and personal-wear patents accounted for less than 50 percent of the total.

This 1923 survey was the last comprehensive study of women's patents by the U.S. government. Save for the applications submitted after ratification of the Nineteenth Amendment, none of these inventors even had the right to vote.

The 5,016 Patents Granted to Women, 1905–21, by Classification, Number, and Percentage

1. **Agriculture, forestry, and animal husbandry: 221 or 4.4 percent**
Poultry, dairy, and stock-raising supplies and equipment; planting, tilling, and harvesting equipment; plant-enemy exterminators; garden tools and equipment.

2. **Mining, quarrying, and metal smelting: 14 or 0.3 percent**

3. Manufacture: 223 or 4.4 percent

Chemical, food, and textile products, processes, and apparatus; foundry materials and apparatus, machine shop and other metalworking tools and devices; leather and shoemaking processes, machines, and tools; power machinery.

4. Structural equipment and materials: 208 or 4.2 percent

Road, conduit, and masonry construction and materials; housebuilding parts, materials, and tools; heating and lighting equipment and appurtenances.

5. Transportation: 345 or 6.9 percent

Automobile accessories, bodies, parts, tires, and tire attachments; bicycles, motorcycles, air-pressure-operated vehicles and parts; horse-drawn vehicles and equipment for horses and vehicles; steam and street railways and equipment; traffic signals and indicators, boats and ship equipment; aircraft and equipment.

6. Trade: 71 or 1.4 percent

Store equipment and furnishings, advertising devices, and equipment; measuring and dispensing devices.

7. Hotel and restaurant equipment: 10 or 0.2 percent

8. Steam laundry, dyeing, and cleaning equipment: 6 or 0.1 percent

9. Dressmakers' and milliners' supplies: 118 or 2.4 percent

10. Office supplies and equipment: 71 or 1.4 percent

11. Fishing: 9 or 0.2 percent

12. Household: 1,385 or 27.6 percent

Kitchen, laundry, dining room, bathroom, bedroom, and nursery equipment; ash, garbage, and trash receptacles; furniture, furnishings, and parts; hangers, brackets, and other household hardware; clothes closet conveniences and garment containers; insect and rodent catchers; and sewing and knitting containers and conveniences.

13. Miscellaneous supplies and equipment: 378 or 7.5 percent

Cutlery, tools, hardware, electrical equipment, glass and earthenware, sewing and embroidery machines, telephone and telegraphic equipment, stationery supplies and equipment, and various devices for wrapping, packing, carrying, or mailing.

14. Scientific instruments: 76 or 1.5 percent

Laboratory equipment; meters; scales; watches; optical and photographic equipment.

15. Ordnance, firearms, and ammunition: 22 or 0.4 percent

16. Personal wear and use: 1,090 or 21.7 percent

Under and outer garments; head-, hand-, and footwear; baby garments; jewelry, toilet articles, purses, umbrellas, and trunks.

17. Beauty parlor and barber supplies: 46 or 0.9 percent

18. Medical, surgical, and dental equipment: 227 or 4.5 percent

19. Safety and sanitation: 129 or 2.6 percent

Property protection devices; life and limb protective gear; sanitation equipment.

20. Education: 75 or 1.5 percent

Mechanical aids to teaching; school furniture and equipment; musical instruction aids.

21. Arts and crafts: 67 or 1.3 percent

Musical instruments and parts; artists' and sculptors' devices; fabric and other craftwork equipment; theater apparatuses.

22. Amusement: 211 or 4.2 percent

Toys; adult games; athletic and camping equipment.

23. Other: 14 or 0.3 percent

Election and registration conveniences; church and burial equipment.

APPENDIX 2

Kids' Stuff

THE DESIGNATION OF youngest woman to receive a U.S. patent is generally—and wrongly—attributed to Betty Galloway, of Georgetown, South Carolina, who was awarded Patent No. 3,395,481 on August 6, 1968. She was ten years old when the patent was issued, and the invention was an appropriate one for her age: a bubblemaking toy.

In reality, the honor goes to sisters Teresa and Mary Thompson, who were only eight and nine, respectively, when they invented and patented a "solar teepee" for a science fair project in 1960. They called the device a Wigwarm and got the idea by watching their father, who was constructing a solar-heated home for the family at the time. The girls wanted a personal version for camping in the backyard.

Wendy Jonnecheck was in the fifth grade when she invented and patented a new style of jump rope, which went on to be manufactured and marketed by Quality Industries of Hillsdale, Michigan.

Thanks to an annual contest now being held by the scholastic publication *My Weekly Reader,* Betty, Wendy, and the Thompsons will be having more competition in the years to come. More than eighty thousand entries were received for the magazine's first national young inventors' contest, which was held in 1986.* According to Dr. Terry Borton, editor-in-chief of *My Weekly Reader,* the contest was conceived because "as a nation, we need to develop inventive talent among our youth." The Japanese have been conducting a national invention contest for children since 1946 and attribute the country's high level of inventiveness in part to that contest.

The grand prize winner of *My Weekly Reader's* first competition was first-grader Suzie Amling, of Auburn, Alabama. Seven-year-old Suzie won a $500 gift certificate and a trip to Washington, D.C. (for herself and her family), for her invention, the "line-leader and keeper."

Suzie's first-grade class walks two thirds of a mile along a busy road

---

*For more information, contact the magazine at 245 Long Hill Road, Middletown, Connecticut 06457.

to get to the public library, and Suzie was often concerned about the safety of her classmates. With the assistance of her father, a horticulture professor at Auburn University, Suzie designed her line-leader and keeper from a length of rope and wire and a number of old suitcase handles. Each student grabs on to a handle, which is electrically connected to the teacher's little black box. Should a student get separated from the pack and let go of the handle, the teacher's black box buzzes a warning signal. The purpose of the invention, as Miss Amling put it simply, is "to keep children together."

The youngest prizewinner in the 1986 contest was Katie Harding, age five. The Bloomington, Indiana, kindergartener never did like those dark winter mornings when her seven-year-old brother walked her down the driveway to catch the school bus. She was forever stepping in mud puddles that she couldn't see; once, her brother, Lee, had to miss a day at school because he stepped in such a large one. "I thought a light on his umbrella would be good," said Katie.

With her mother's help, Katie attached a flashlight to an umbrella, creating the "mud puddle spotter." The invention earned her a $250 savings bond and front-page coverage in her local newspaper.

All of twelve, Anna Thompson of Craig, Colorado, won the sixth-grade division for her "measure quick shortening dispenser," a device to help with the tricky task of measuring solid shortening into a recipe. The measure quick shortening dispenser uses disposable plastic bags that fit onto a cylinder, which then squeezes out the appropriate quantity of shortening into a convenient package.

Another invention by a twelve-year-old girl went on to be patented and became the basis of a profitable manufacturing company. Becky Schroeder of Toledo, Ohio, conceived the Glo-Sheet when she was ten, patented it at twelve, and had a going concern by the time she was twenty-two.

It started one evening when young Becky was sitting in the parked family car, waiting for her mother to return from an errand. Becky had homework to do and thought, "Wouldn't it be neat if there was some way to write in the dark? Maybe there's some way to 'light up' writing paper."

With the encouragement of her father—who just happened to be a patent attorney—Becky researched phosphorescent materials. In two years, she held Patent No. 3,832,556 for her Glo-Sheet, an acrylic board that illuminates the sheet of paper placed on top of it. In 1975 Patent No. 3,879,611 was granted for refinements of the concept.

"If one attempts to write in the dark," said Becky in her patent application, "I have found that although the mechanics of writing can be accomplished with little more than usual effort, writing in straight lines with uniform spacing between lines and without overlap is difficult in the absence of some guide means. According to my present invention, I have found that guide lines for material written in the dark can be provided with very little light. . . . Furthermore, I have found that when a sheet, to which lines of commercially available phosphorescent paint is applied, is charged by even a brief exposure to light, may be seen clearly in the dark through one or more sheets of ordinary writing paper."

Becky's research into chemiluminescent and bioluminescent materials taught her that there are many inexpensive substances that, when exposed even momentarily to sunlight or a bright light bulb, will continue to glow softly for fifteen minutes or more. Her Glo-Sheet allowed two different kinds of backlight. In one version, the whole board shines softly. In another, only the guide lines can be seen through the user's worksheet—like the frontispiece that comes with pads of plain notepaper.

In the following decade, Miss Schroeder received ten more patents for improvements to the Glo-Sheet. By the time she graduated from college in 1983, she was the owner and operator of B. J. Products, Inc., which manufactures and markets the Glo-Sheet. She sells the items to police departments, hospitals, and the U.S. Navy, and even is negotiating with NASA.

APPENDIX 3

Obtaining a Patent

THERE HAVE BEEN inventors and inventions long before there were patents. Before 1624, when the British Parliament established the modern-day patent system, inventors had little protection under the law. Anyone who wanted to could make, market, and derive income from the innovations of another. Giving manufacturing rights to the latest hot product, in fact, was a common form of royal favoritism. Tired of the king awarding exclusive rights to "any new manner of manufacture" to his cronies, Parliament declared that henceforth patents would be awarded to the actual inventor.

As well as being fair and ethical, the new patent system had the positive effect of promoting technological advancement: The possibility of financial reward is a powerful incentive. The patent system no doubt helped to usher in the Industrial Revolution by ensuring inventors an adequate return on their creations

The U.S. patent system is based on England's. More than four million U.S. patents have been filed since the first was granted to Samuel Hopkins on July 31, 1790. For most of the nineteenth century, the U.S. Patent Office required the submission of a three-dimensional model along with a patent application. The model requirement was dropped in 1880—partially because the scientific establishment was recognizing the concept of "intellectual property," or patentable ideas, and partially because the patent office was simply inundated with mechanical contraptions.

In his speech dedicating a new Patent Office in 1900, President William McKinley said, "Everything that can possibly be invented has been invented." Millions of patents later, we know that the chief executive's observation was, ah, patently ridiculous.

Today about eighty thousand patents are filed annually. Although you no longer have to be handy in modelmaking, the patent filing process is nevertheless considerably more complex, time-consuming, and expensive than it was a hundred years ago. Not all inventions are patentable, so it's best to think twice whether you actually need a patent before setting the U.S. Patent Office's wheels in motion.

A patent is a license that the federal government issues to protect an inventor from having others copy and sell her or his invention in the United States, its territories, and its possessions. To be patentable, an invention must be "new," which the U.S. Patent Office defines as (1) not already in public use, (2) not previously described in a printed publication, and (3) not so obvious that a person of ordinary skills could make it. (This last qualifier is trickier than it sounds; the reason that Eli Whitney—and by extension, Catherine Greene—did not make more money from the cotton gin was that its patent was ignored wholesale by southern planters, who claimed the device was so simple as to be obvious to anyone.)

The most difficult part of the patent-granting process is the prerequisite patent search. Anyone with $65 can *file* for a patent. If the patent is granted, there's an additional "issue fee" of $100, and then still another cost for printing charges (approximately $75 at present). But the Patent Office will grant your patent only after it's convinced that someone hasn't already beaten you to the punch.

Theoretically, anyone can conduct a patent search on their own, but the enormity of the task prompts most people to hire a registered patent attorney to sift through those four-million-plus prior licenses. The Patent Office can provide you with a list of patent attorneys in your area.

Once you file a patent, expect two years to pass before it's issued. You've then got seventeen years left during which to market your invention in luxurious exclusivity; after that, it's released to the public domain. The only way a patent can be extended is literally by an act of Congress.

For more information on patents, contact:

> Office of Information
> U.S. Patent Office
> Washington, D.C.   20231

And good luck!

Index